Horatius Bonar

Hymns of Faith and Hope

Volume 2

Horatius Bonar

Hymns of Faith and Hope
Volume 2

ISBN/EAN: 9783337091323

Printed in Europe, USA, Canada, Australia, Japan

Cover: Foto ©Lupo / pixelio.de

More available books at **www.hansebooks.com**

HYMNS

OF

FAITH AND HOPE.

BY

HORATIUS BONAR, D.D.,

AUTHOR OF THE "NIGHT OF WEEPING," "THE MORNING OF JOY," ETC.

NEW YORK:

ROBERT CARTER & BROTHERS,

No. 530 BROADWAY.

1864.

Contents.

CONTENTS.

HYMNS OF FAITH AND HOPE.

DIVINE ORDER.

'Tis first the true and then the beautiful,
　　Not first the beautiful and then the true;
First the wild moor, with rock and reed and pool,
　　Then the gay garden, rich in scent and hue.

'Tis first the good and then the beautiful,—
　　Not first the beautiful and then the good;
First the rough seed, sown in the rougher soil,
　　Then the flower-blossom, or the branching wood.

Not first the glad and then the sorrowful,—
　　But first the sorrowful, and then the glad;
Tears for a day,—for earth of tears is full,
　　Then we forget that we were ever sad.

Not first the bright, and after that the dark,—
    But first the dark, and after that the bright;
First the thick cloud, and then the rainbow's arc,
    First the dark grave, then resurrection-light.

'Tis first the night,—stern night of storm and war,—
    Long nights of heavy clouds and veiled skies;
Then the far sparkle of the Morning-star,
    That bids the saints awake and dawn arise.

LEFT BEHIND.

Look at this starbeam ! From its place of birth,
   It has come down to greet us here below ;
Now it alights unwearied on this earth,
   Nor storm nor night have quenched its heavenly
      glow.

Unbent before the winter's rugged blast,
   Unsoiled by this sad planet's tainted air,
It sparkles out from yon unmeasured vast,
   Bright 'mid the brightest, 'mid the fairest fair.

Undimmed it reaches me ; but yet alone :
   The thousand gay companions that took wing
Along with it have perished one by one,
   Scattered o'er space like blossoms of the spring.

Some to yon nearer orbs have sped their course,
   Yon city's smoke has quenched a thousand more ;
Myriads in yon dark cloud have spent their force ;
   A few stray gleams are all that reach our shore.

And with us! How many, who began
    Life's race with us, are dropping by the way ;
Losing themselves in darkness one by one,
    From the glad goal departing wide astray !

When we shall reach the kingdom of the blest,
    How few who started with us shall we find
Arriving or arrived, for glorious rest !
    How many shall we mourn as left behind !*

    " Pauci læta arva tenemus."— *Virgil, Æneid,* **VI.**

THE MEETING-PLACE.

Where the faded flower shall freshen,—
Freshen never more to fade;
Where the shaded sky shall brighten,—
Brighten never more to shade:
Where the sun-blaze never scorches;
Where the star-beams cease to chill;
Where no tempest stirs the echoes
Of the wood, or wave, or hill:
Where the morn shall wake in gladness,
And the moon the joy prolong,
Where the daylight dies in fragrance,
'Mid the burst of holy song:
      Brother, we shall meet and rest
      'Mid the holy and the blest!

Where no shadow shall bewilder,
Where life's vain parade is o'er,
Where the sleep of sin is broken,
And the dreamer dreams no more:

Where the bond is never severed ;—
   Partings, claspings, sob and moan,
Midnight waking, twilight weeping,
   Heavy noontide,—all are done :
Where the child has found its mother,
   Where the mother finds the child,
Where dear families are gathered,
   That were scattered on the wild :
      Brother, we shall meet and rest
      'Mid the holy and the blest !

Where the hidden wound is healed,
   Where the blighted light re-blooms,
Where the smitten heart the freshness
   Of its buoyant youth resumes :
Where the love that here we lavish
   On the withering leaves of time,
Shall have fadeless flowers to fix on
   In an ever spring bright clime :
Where we find the joy of loving,
   As we never loved before,—
Loving on, unchilled, unhindered,
   Loving once and evermore :
      Brother, we shall meet and rest,
      'Mid the holy and the blest !

Where a blasted world shall brighten
   Underneath a bluer sphere,
And a softer, gentler sunshine
   Shed its healing splendor here :
Where earth's barren vales shall blossom,
   Putting on their robe of green,
And a purer, fairer Eden
   Be where only wastes have been :
Where a King in kingly glory,
   Such as earth has never known,
Shall assume the righteous sceptre,
   Claim and wear the holy crown :
      Brother, we shall meet and rest,
      'Mid the holy and the blest.

A STRANGER HERE.

I miss the dear paternal dwelling,
  Which mem'ry, still undimmed, recals,
A thousand early stories telling;
  I miss the venerable walls.

I miss the chamber of my childhood,
  I miss the shade of boyhood's tree,—
The glen, the path, the cliff, the wild-wood,
  The music of the well-known sea.

I miss the ivied haunt of moonlight,
  I miss the forest and the stream,
I miss the fragrant grove of noonlight,
  I miss our mountain's sunset gleam.

I miss the green slope, where, reposing,
  I mused upon the near and far,
Marked, one by one, each floweret closing,
  Watched, one by one, each opening star

I miss the well-remembered faces,
   The voices, forms, of fresher days ;
Time ploughs not up these deep-drawn traces,
   These lines no ages can erase.

I miss them all, for, unforgetting,
   My spirit o'er the past still strays,
And, much its wasted years regretting,
   It treads again these shaded ways.

I mourn not that each early token
   Is now to me a faded flower,
Nor that the magic snare is broken
   That held me with its mystic power.

I murmur not that now a stranger
   I pass along the smiling earth ;
I know the snare, I dread the danger,
   I hate the haunts, I shun the mirth.

My hopes are passing upward, onward,
   And with my hopes my heart has gone ;
My eye is turning skyward, sunward,
   Where glory brightens round yon throne.

My spirit seeks its dwelling yonder;
   And fate fore-dates the joyful day
When these old skies shall cease to sunder
   The one dear love-linked family.

Well-pleased I find years rolling o'er me,
   And hear each day-time's measured tread;
Far fewer clouds now stretch before me,
   Behind me is the darkness spread.

And summer's suns are swiftly setting,
   And life moves downward in their train,
And autumn dews are fondly wetting
   The faded cheek of earth in vain.

December moons are coldly waning,
   And life with them is on the wane;
Storm-laden skies with sad complaining,
   Bend blackly o'er the unsmiling main.

My future from my past unlinking,
   Each dying year untwines the spell;
The visible is swiftly sinking,
   Uprises the invisible.

To light, unchanging, and eternal,
   From mists that sadden this bleak waste,
To scenes that smile for ever vernal,
   From winter's blackening leaf I haste.

Earth, what a sorrow lies before thee,
   None like it in the shadowy past ;—
The sharpest throe that ever tore thee,
   Even tho' the briefest and the last !

I see the fair moon veil her lustre,
   I see the sackcloth of the sun ;
The shrouding of each starry cluster,
   The threefold woe of earth begun.

I see the shadows of its sunset ;
   And wrapped in these the Avenger's form ,
I see the Armageddon-onset ;
   But I shall be above the storm.

There comes the moaning and the sighing,
   There comes the hot tear's heavy fall,
The thousand agonies of dying ;—
   But I shall! be beyond them all.

OCEAN TEACHINGS.

"This great and wide sea."—PSALM civ. 25.

THAT rising storm !   It has awakened me ;
  My slumbering spirit starts to life anew ;
That blinding spray-drift, how it falls upon me,
  As on the weary flower the freshening dew.

That rugged rock-fringe that girds in the ocean,
  And calls the foam from its translucent blue,
It seems to pour strange strength into my spirit,—
  Strength for endurance, strength for conflict too.

And these bright ocean-birds, these billow-rangers,
  The snowy-breasted,—each a winged wave—
They tell me how to joy in storm and dangers,
  When surges whiten, or when whirlwinds rave.

And these green-stretching fields, these peaceful hol-
      lows,
  That hear the tempest, but take no alarm,

Has not their placid verdure sweetly taught me
　The peace within when all without is storm ?

And thou keen sun-flash, through the cloud-wreath
　　bursting,
　Silvering the sea, the sward, the rock, the foam,
What light within me has thy pure gleam kindled ?
　'Tis from the land of light that thou art come.

And of the time how blithely art thou telling,
　When cloud and change and tempest shall take
　　wing ;
Each beam of thine prophetic of the glory,
　Creation's daybreak, earth's long-promised spring.

Even thus it is, my God me daily teacheth
　Sweet knowledge out of all I hear and see ;
Each object has a heavenly voice within it,
　Each scene, however troubled, speaks to me.

For all upon this earth is broken beauty,
　Yet out of all what strange, deep lessons rise ?
Each hour is giving out its heaven-sent wisdom,
　A message from the sea, the shore, the skies.

NO MORE SEA.

Καὶ ἡ θάλασσα οὐκ ἔστιν ἔτι.—(REV. xxi. 1.)

SUMMER Ocean, idly washing
　　This grey rock on which I lean;
Summer Ocean, broadly flashing
　　With thy hues of gold and green;
Gently swelling, wildly dashing
　　O'er yon island-studded scene;
Summer Ocean, how I'll miss thee,—
　　Miss the thunder of thy roar,
Miss the music of thy ripple,
　　Miss thy sorrow-soothing shore,-
Summer Ocean, how I'll miss thee,
　　When "the sea shall be no more."
Summer Ocean, how I'll miss thee,
　　As along thy strand I range;
Or as here I sit and watch thee
　　In thy moods of endless change—

Mirthful moods of morning gladness,
Musing moods of sunset sadness;
When the dying winds caress thee,
And the sinking sunbeams kiss thee,
And the crimson cloudlets press thee,
And all nature seems to bless thee !—
Summer Ocean, how I 'll miss thee,—
Miss the wonders of thy shore,
Miss the magic of thy grandeur,
When "the sea shall be no more !"

And yet sometimes in my musings,
When I think of what shall be ;
In the day of earth's new glory,
Still I seem to roam by thee.
As if all had not departed,
But the glory lingered still ;
As if that which made thee lovely,
Had remained unchangeable.
Only that which marred thy beauty,—
Only *that* had passed away,
Sullen wilds of Ocean-moorland,
Bloated features of decay.
Only that dark waste of waters,

Line ne' er fathomed, eye ne 'er scanned,
Only *that* shall shrink and vanish,
   Yielding back the imprisoned land.
Yielding back earth's fertile hollows,
   Long submerged and hidden plains;
Giving up a thousand valleys,
   Of the ancient world's domains.
Leaving still bright azure ranges,
   Winding round this rocky tower;
Leaving still yon gem-bright island,
   Sparkling like an ocean-flower.
Leaving still some placid stretches,
   Where the sunbeams bathe at noon,
Leaving still some lake-like reaches,
   Mirrors for the silver moon.
Only all of gloom and horror,
   Idle wastes of endless brine,
Haunts of darkness, storm, and danger,
   These shall be no longer thine.
Backward ebbing, wave and ripple,
   Wondrous scenes shall then disclose
And, like earth's, the wastes of ocean
   Then shall blossom as the rose.

THE CHANGE.

I LOVE yon pale blue sky; it is the floor
    Of that glad home where I shall shortly be;
A home from which I shall go out no more;
    From toil and grief and vanity set free.

I gaze upon yon everlasting arch,
    Up which the bright stars wander, as they shine;
And as I mark them in their nightly march,
    I think how soon that journey shall be mine!

Yon silver drift of silent cloud, far up
    In the still heaven—through you my pathway lies;
Yon rugged mountain-peak—how soon your top
    Shall I behold beneath me, as I rise!

Not many more of life's slow-pacing hours,
    Shaded with sorrow's melancholy hue;—
Oh, what a glad ascending shall be ours,
    Oh, what a pathway up yon starry blue!

3

A journey like Elijah's, swift and bright,
 Caught gently upward to an early crown,
In heaven's own chariot of unblazing light,*
 With death untasted and the grave unknown.

THE CLOUDLESS.

No shadows yonder !
 All light and song ;
Each day I wonder,
 And say, How long
Shall time me sunder
 From that dear throng ?

No weeping yonder !
 All fled away ;
While here I wander
 Each weary day,
And sigh as I ponder
 My long, long stay.

* Θειῳ πυρὶ παμφαὴς.—Soph. Philoct.

No partings yonder!
  Time and space never
Again shall sunder;
  Hearts cannot sever;
Dearer and fonder
  Hands clasp for ever.*

None wanting yonder,
  Bought by the Lamb!
All gathered under
  The evergreen palm;
Loud as night's thunder
  Ascends the glad psalm.

* 'A λικρυν νεμονται αιῶνα.—Pindar. Olymp.

THE HOME SICKNESS.

"O civitas sancta, civitas speciosa, de longinquo te saluto, ad te clamo, te requiro."—*Augustine, De Spir. et Anim.*

AND whence this weariness,
 This gathering cloud of gloom ?
Whence this dull weight of loneliness,
 These greedy cravings for the tomb ?
These greedier cravings for the hopes that lie
Beyond the tomb, beyond the things that die ;
Beyond the smiles and joys that come and go,
Fevering the spirit with their fitful flow ;
Beyond the circle where the shadows fall ;
Within the region where my God is all.

It is not that I fear
 To breast the storm or wrestle with the wave,
 To swim the torrent or the blast to brave,
 To toil or suffer in this day of strife
 As He may will who gave this struggling life,—
But I am homesick !

It is not that the cross
    Is heavier than this drooping frame can bear,
    Or that I find no kindred heart to share
    The burden, which, in these last days of ill,
    Seems to press heavier, sharper, sorer still,—
But I am homesick!

It is not that the snare
    Is laid around for my unwary feet,
    And that a thousand wily tempters greet
    My slippery steps and lead me far astray
    From that safe guidance of the narrow way,—
But I am homesick!

It is not that the path
    Is rough and perilous, beset with foes,
    From the first step down to its weary close,
    Strewn with the flint, the briar, and the thorn,
    That wound my limbs and leave my raiment torn,
But I am homesick!

It is not that the sky
    Is darkly sad, and the unloving air
    Chills me to fainting; and the clouds that there
3*

Hang over me seem signal clouds unfurled,
Portending wrath to an unready world,—
But I am homesick !

It is not that the earth
    Has grown less bright and fair,—that these grey
        hills,
    These ever-lapsing, ever-lulling rills,
    And these breeze-haunted woods, that ocean clear,
    Have now become less beautiful, less dear,—
But I am homesick !

    Let me, then, weary be !
        I shrink not,—murmur not ;
    In all this homelessness I see
        The Church's pilgrim-lot ;
    Her lot until her absent Lord shall come,
    And the long homeless here, shall find a home.

    Then no more weariness !
        No gathering cloud of gloom ;
    Then no dull weight of loneliness,
        No greedy cravings for the tomb :
    For death shall then be swallowed up of life,
    And the glad victory shall end the strife !

THE LAND OF LIGHT.

THAT clime is not like this dull clime of ours;
    All, all is brightness there;
A sweeter influence breathes around its flowers,
    And a far milder air.
No calm below is like that calm above.
No region here is like that realm of love;
Earth's softest spring ne'er shed so soft a light,
Earth's brightest summer never shone so bright.

That sky is not like this sad sky of ours,
    Tinged with earth's change and care:
No shadow dims it, and no rain-cloud lowers,—
    No broken sunshine there!
One everlasting stretch of azure pours
Its stainless splendor o'er these sinless shores;
For there Jehovah shines with heavenly ray,
There Jesus reigns dispensing endless day.

Those dwellers there are not like these of earth,
    No mortal stain they bear ;
And yet they seem of kindred blood and birth,—
    Whence, and how came they there?
Earth was their native soil, from sin and shame,
Through tribulation they to glory came ;
Bond-slaves delivered from sin's crushing load,
Brands plucked from burning by the hand of God.

Those robes of theirs are not for these below ;
    No angel's half so bright !
Whence came that beauty, whence that living glow !
    Whence came that radiant white ?
Washed in the blood of the atoning Lamb,
Fair as the light those robes of theirs became,
And now, all tears wiped off from every eye,
They wander where the freshest pastures lie,
Through all the nightless day of that unfading
    sky !

THE SEEN AND THE UNSEEN.

On the Great Exhibition, 1851.

Ha! yon burst of crystal splendor,
  Sunlight, starlight, blent in one;
Starlight set in arctic azure,
  Sunlight from the burning zone!
Gold and silver, gems and marble,
  All creation's jewelry;
Earth's uncovered waste of riches,
  Treasures of the ancient sea.
      Heir of glory,
  What is that to thee and me?

Iris and Aurora braided—
  How the woven colors shine!
Snow-gleams from an Alpine summit,
  Torch-light from a spar-roofed mine.

Like Arabia's matchless palace,
  Child of magic's strong decree,
One vast globe of living sapphire,
  Floor, walls, columns, canopy.
      Heir of glory,
  What is that to thee and me?

Forms of beauty, shapes of wonder,
  Trophies of triumphant toil;
Never Athens, Rome, Palmyra,
  Gazed on such a costly spoil.
Dazzling the bewildered vision,
  More than princely pomp we see;
What the blaze of the Alhambra,
  Dome of emerald, to thee?
      Heir of glory,
  What is that to thee and me?

Farthest cities pour their riches,
  Farthest empires muster here,
Art her jubilee proclaiming
  To the nations far and near.

From the crowd in wonder gazing,
    Science claims the prostrate knee;
This her temple, diamond-blazing,
    Shrine of her idolatry.
      Heir of glory,
  What is that to thee and me?

Listen to her tale of wonder,
    Of her plastic, potent spell;
'T is a big and braggart story,
    Yet she tells it fair and well.
She the gifted, gay magician,
    Mistress of earth, air, and sea;
This majestic apparition,
    Offspring of her sorcery.
      Heir of glory,
  What is that to thee and me?

What to that for which we 're waiting
    Is this glittering earthly toy?
Heavenly glory, holy splendor,
    Sum of grandeur, sum of joy.

Not the gems that time can tarnish,
  Not the hues that dim and die,
Not the glow that cheats the lover,
  Shaded with mortality.
     Heir of glory,
  That shall be for thee and me!

Not the light that leaves us darker,
  Nor the gleams that come and go,
Not the mirth whose end is madness,
  Not the joy whose fruit is woe;
Not the notes that die at sunset,
  Not the fashion of a day;
But the everlasting beauty,
  And the endless melody.
     Heir of glory,
  That shall be for thee and me!

City of the pearl-bright portal;
  City of the jasper wall;
City of the golden pavement;
  Seat of endless festival.

City of Jehovah, Salem,
　　City of eternity,
To thy bridal-hall of gladness,
　　From this prison would I flee.
　　　　Heir of glory,
　That shall be for thee and me!

Ah! with such strange spells around me,
　　Fairest of what earth calls fair,
How I need thy fairer image,
　　To undo the syren snare?
Lest the subtle serpent-tempter
　　Lure me with his radiant lie;
As if sin were sin no longer,
　　Life were no more vanity.
　　　　Heir of glory,
　What is that to thee and me?

Yes, I need *thee*, heavenly city,
　　My low spirit to upbear;
Yes, I need thee—earth's enchantments
　　So beguile me with their glare.

Let me see thee, then these fetters
    Break asunder; I am free;
Then this pomp no longer chains me;
    Faith has won the victory.
        Heir of glory,
    That shall be for thee and me!

Soon where earthly beauty blinds not,
    No excess of brilliance palls,
Salem, city of the holy,
    We shall be within thy walls!
There, beside yon crystal river,
    There, beneath life's wondrous tree,
There, with naught to cloud or sever—
    Ever with the Lamb to be!
        Heir of glory,
    That shall be for thee and me!

ADVENT.

THE Church has waited long
    Her absent Lord to see;
And still in loneliness she waits,
    A friendless stranger she.
Age after age has gone,
    Sun after sun has set,
And still in weeds of widowhood
    She weeps a mourner yet.
        Come, then, Lord Jesus, come !

Saint after saint on earth
    Has lived, and loved, and died ;
And as they left us one by one,
    We laid them side by side ;
We laid them down to sleep,
    But not in hope forlorn ;
We laid them but to ripen there,
    Till the last glorious morn.
        Came, then, Lord Jesus, come !

The serpent's brood increase,
　　The powers of hell grow bold,
The conflict thickens, faith is low,
　　And love is waxing cold.
How long, O Lord our God,
　　Holy and true, and good,
Wilt Thou not judge Thy suffering Church,
　　Her sighs and tears and blood ?
　　　　Come, then, Lord Jesus, come !

We long to hear Thy voice,
　　To see Thee face to face,
To share Thy crown and glory then,
　　As now we share Thy grace.
Should not the loving bride
　　The absent bridegroom mourn ?
Should she not wear the weeds of grief
　　Until her Lord return ?
　　　　Come, then, Lord Jesus, come

The whole creation groans,
　　And waits to hear that voice,
That shall restore her comeliness,
　　And make her wastes rejoice.

Come, Lord, and wipe away
  The curse, the sin, the stain,
Aud make this blighted world of ours
  Thine own fair world again.
    Come, then, Lord Jesus, come!

DAWN.

LIGHT of the better morning,
  Shine down on me!
Sun of the brighter heaven,
  Bid darkness flee!
Thy warmth impart
To this dull heart:
Pour in thy light,
And let this night
Be turned to day
By thy mild ray!
  Lord Jesus, come;
    Thou day-star shine;
  Enlighten now
    This soul of mine!
     4*

Streaks of the better dawning
 Break on my sight,
Fringing with silver edges
 These clouds of night.
Gems on morn's brow,
Glow, brightly glow,
Foretelling soon
The ascending noon,
Wakening this earth
To second birth,
 When He shall come
  To earth again,
 Who comes to judge,
  Who comes to reign.

RETURN UNTO THY REST.

Cease, my soul, thy strayings!
　　Have they brought thee peace?
Come, no more delayings,
　　Cease thy wanderings, cease.
　　　　These vanities how vain!
　　　　Wander not again.

Thou hast found thy centre;
　　There, my soul, abide;
Never more adventure
　　Now to swerve aside.
　　　　These vanities how vain!
　　　　Wander not again.

Thou hast reached thy dwelling;
　　Safe, sure anchorage
From the perilous swelling
　　Of the tempest's rage.
　　　　These vanities how vain!
　　　　Wander not again.

Tranquil hours now greet thee,
   In thy calm abode;
Gracious looks now meet thee,
   From thy loving God.
      These vanities how vain!
      Wander not again.

See yon star, love-lighted,
   Sparkles from on high;
See yon hope, love-plighted,
   Cheers thy heaviest sky.
      These vanities how vain!
      Wander not again.

Watch, my soul, the glory
   Coming brightly up,
O'er yon forest hoary,
   O'er yon mountain-top.
      These vanities how vain!
      Wander not again.

'Tis the bridal morning;
   Rise, make no delay;

Put on thine adorning,
  Cast thy weeds away.
     These vanities how vain!
     Wander not again.

Pierce these mists that blind thee,
  Press to yonder prize,
Break the bonds that bind thee,
  Rise, my soul, arise!
     These vanities how vain!
     Wander not again.

THE MORNING STAR.

THERE is a morning star, my soul,
   There is a morning star;
'Twill soon be near and bright, tho' now
   It seems so dim and far.
And when time's stars have come and gone
And every mist of earth has flown,
That better star shall rise
On this world's clouded skies,
          To shine forever!

The night is well nigh spent, my soul,
   The night is well nigh spent,
And soon above our heads shall shine
   A glorious firmament:
A sky all glad, and pure, and bright,
The Lamb, once slain, its perfect light
A star without a cloud,
Whose light no mists enshroud,
          Descending never.

THINGS HOPED FOR.

THESE are the crowns that we shall wear
   When all thy saints are crowned ;
These are the palms that we shall bear
   On yonder holy ground.   .

Far off as yet, reserved in heaven,
   Above that veiling sky,
They sparkle, like the stars of even,
   To hope's far-piercing eye.

These are the robes, unsoiled and white,
   Which then we shall put on,
When, foremost 'mong the sons of light,
   We sit on yonder throne.

That city with the jewelled crest,
   Like some new-lighted sun ;
A blaze of burning amethyst—
   Ten thousand orbs in one ;—

That is the city of the saints,
   Where we so soon shall stand,
When we shall strike these desert-tents,
   And quit this desert-sand.

These are the everlasting hills,
   With summits bathed in day :
The slopes down which the living rills,
   Soft-lapsing, take their way.

Fair vision ! how thy distant gleam
   Brightens time's saddest hue ;
Far fairer than the fairest dream,
   · And yet so strangely true !

Fair vision ! how thou liftest up
   The drooping brow and eye ;
With the calm joy of thy sure hope
   Fixing our souls on high.

Thy light makes even the darkest page
   In memory's scroll grow fair ;
Blanching the lines which tears and age
   Had only deepened there.

With thee in view, the rugged slope
   Becomes a level way,
Smoothed by the magic of thy hope,
   And gladdened by thy ray.

With thee in view, how poor appear
   The world's most winning smiles;
Vain is the tempter's subtlest snare,
   And vain hell's varied wiles.

Time's glory fades; its beauty now
   Has ceased to lure or blind;
Each gay enchantment here below
   Has lost its power to bind.

Then welcome toil, and care, and pain !
   And welcome sorrow too !
All toil is rest, all grief is gain,
   With such a prize in view.

Come crown and throne, come robe and palm !
   Burst forth glad stream of peace !
Come, holy city of the Lamb !
   Rise, Sun of Righteousness !

When shall the clouds that veil thy rays
   Forever be withdrawn?
Why dost thou tarry, day of days?
   When shall thy gladness dawn?

THROUGH DEATH TO LIFE

THE star is not extinguished when it sets
   Upon the dull horizon; it but goes
To shine in other skies, then re-appear
   In ours, as fresh as when it first arose.

The river is not lost, when, o'er the rock,
   It pours its flood into the abyss below:
Its scattered force re-gathering from the shock,
   It hastens onward, with yet fuller flow.

The bright sun dies not, when the shadowing orb
   Of the eclipsing moon obscures its ray:
It still is shining on; and soon to us
   Will burst undimmed into the joy of day.

The lily dies not, when both flower and leaf
    Fade, and are strewed upon the chill sad ground;
Gone down for shelter to its mother-earth,
    'Twill rise, re-bloom, and shed its fragrance
    round.

The dew-drop dies not, when it leaves the flower,
    And passes upward on the beam of morn;
It does but hide itself in light on high,
    To its loved flower at twilight to return.

The fine gold has not perished, when the flame
    Seizes upon it with consuming glow;
In freshened splendor it comes forth anew,
    To sparkle on the monarch's throne or brow.

Thus nothing dies, or only dies to live:
    Star, stream, sun, flower, the dew-drop, and the
    gold;
Each goodly thing, instinct with buoyant hope,
    Hastes to put on its purer, finer mould.

Thus in the quiet joy of kindly trust,
    We bid each parting saint a brief farewell;

Weeping, yet smiling, we commit their dust
   To the safe keeping of the silent cell.

Softly within that peaceful resting-place
   We lay their wearied limbs, and bid the clay
Press lightly on them till the night be past,
   And the far east give note of coming day.

The day of re-appearing! how it speeds!
   He who is true and faithful speaks the word.
Then shall we ever be with those we love—
   Then shall we be for ever with the Lord.

The shout is heard; the archangel's voice goes
     forth ;
   The trumpet sounds; the dead awake and sing ;
The living put on glory ; one glad band,
   They hasten up to meet their coming King.

Short death and darkness! Endless life and light!
   Short dimming ; endless shining in yon sphere,
Where all is incorruptible and pure ;—
   The joy without the pain, the smile without the
     tear.

HORA NOVISSIMA.

FAR down the ages now,
   Her journey well-nigh done,
The pilgrim Church pursues her way,
   In haste to reach the crown.

The story of the past
   Comes up before her view;
How well it seems to suit her still,
   Old, and yet ever new.

'Tis the same story still,
   Of sin and weariness,
Of grace and love still flowing down
   To pardon and to bless.

'Tis the old sorrow still,
   The briar and the thorn;
And 'tis the same old solace yet—
   The hope of coming morn.

5*

No wider is the gate,
  No broader is the way,
No smoother is the ancient path
  That leads to light and day.

No lighter is the load
  Beneath whose weight we cry,
No tamer grows the rebel flesh,
  Nor less our enemy.

No sweeter is the cup,
  Nor less our lot of ill ;
'Twas tribulation ages since,
  'Tis tribulation still.

No greener are the rocks.
  No fresher flow the rills,
No roses in the wilds appear,
  No vines upon the hills.

Still dark the sky above,
  And sharp the desert air ,
'Tis wide, bleak desolation round,
  And shadow everywhere.

Dawn lingers on yon cliff;
   But, oh, how slow to spring!
Morning still nestles on yon wave,
   Afraid to try its wing.

No slacker grows the fight,
   No feebler is the foe,
No less the need of armor tried,
   Of shield, and spear, and bow.

Nor less we feel the blank
   Of earth's still absent King;
Whose presence is of all our bliss
   The everlasting spring.

Thus onward still we press,
   Through evil and through good,
Through pain, and poverty, and want,
   Through peril and through blood.

Still faithful to our God,
   And to our Captain true;
We follow where he leads the way,
   The kingdom in our view.

THE NIGHT COMETH

TIME'S sun is fast setting,
    Its twilight is nigh,
Its evening is falling
    In cloud o'er the sky,
Its shadows are stretching
    In ominous gloom ;
Its midnight approaches,
    The midnight of doom.
Then haste, sinner, haste, there is mercy for thee,
And wrath is preparing,—flee, lingerer, flee !

Rides forth the fierce tempest
    On the wing of the cloud ;
The moan of the night-blast
    Is fitful and loud ;
The mountains are heaving,
    The forests are bowed,
The ocean is surging,
    Earth gathers its shroud.
Then haste, sinner, haste, there is mercy for thee,
And wrath is preparing,—flee, lingerer, flee !

The vision is nearing—
　　The Judge and the throne !—
The voice of the Angel
　　Proclaims " It is done."
On the whirl of the tempest
　　Its ruler shall come,
And the blaze of its glory
　　Flash out from its gloom,—
Then haste, sinner, haste, there is mercy for thee,
And wrath is preparing,—flee, lingerer, flee !

With clouds He is coming !
　　His people shall sing,
With gladness they hail him
　　Redeemer and King.
The iron rod wielding,
　　The rod of his ire,
He cometh to kindle
　　Earth's last fatal fire !
Then haste, sinner, haste, there is mercy for thee,
And wrath is preparing,—-flee, lingerer, flee !

THE DAY AFTER ARMAGEDDON.

"They have blown the trumpet, but none goeth to the battle."—Ezek. vii. 14.

'Tis the summons to battle !
　　But the cry is unheard ;
The trumpet has spoken,
　　Not a warrior has stirred.

Hark, the summons to battle !
　　It has sounded again ;
Still louder and keener ;—
　　It has sounded in vain.

Yet a third time and shriller,
　　That war-note has blown ;
But the answer that cometh
　　Is the echo alone.

'Tis the silence of silence !
   Tower, tent, vale, and hill,
Field, forest, and highway,—
   All soundless and still !

No challenge is lifted,
   No signal unfurled ;
'Tis man's dark hour of terror,
   The awe of the world.

For the arm of Jehovah
   Has been bared in its might,
And the sword of his vengeance
   Has been burnished to smite.

Through the ridges of battle
   His ploughshare has sped ;
And the tents of the living
   Are the tombs of the dead.

The rude roar of millions
   Is hushed in an hour ;
The array of the mighty
   Is crushed in its power.

'Twas man's proudest muster
   Of sinew and steel:
His army of armies,
   Mail-clad to the heel.

No sun had e'er dawned on
   So fearful a day,
No trumpet had marshalled
   So dread an array.

As if earth in her frenzy,
   From each region afar,
Had poured forth her nations
   For the shock of that war.

In the flush of their manhood,
   In the bud of their prime,
In veteran ripeness,—
   The men of each clime

Came thronging and rushing,
   Like rivers in flood,
Defying the terrors
   And vengeance of God.

For the ruler of darkness,
   The God of this world,
Had summoned his armies,
   His banner unfurled.

As the storm-cloud it gathered,
   As the lightning it sped ;
As the mist it has vanished ;—
   All is still as the dead.

Like the desert at midnight,—
   Not a breath nor a beam ;
'Tis the silence of silence,
   The dream of a dream.

Now, chains for the spoiler !
   Dark and swift be his doom !
Thou hast trodden the nations,—
   Thy treading is come !

Earth, cease now thy wailing,
   Thy wounds bleed no more ;
Lo, the curse is departing,
   Thy sorrows are o'er !

Rise, daughter of Judah ;
    Awake now and sing ;
It has come, the glad kingdom,
    He has come, the great King !

Thy long night is ending
    Of sorrow and wrong ;
For shame there is glory,
    For weeping a song.

The new morn is dawning,
    Bursts forth the new sun ;
The new verdure is smiling,
    The new age is begun.

REST YONDER.

This is not my place of resting,
   Mine's a city yet to come;
Onward to it I am hasting—
   On to my eternal home.

In it all is light and glory,
   O'er it shines a nightless day;
Every trace of sin's sad story,
   All the curse, has passed away.

There the Lamb, our Shepherd, leads us,
   By the streams of life along;
On the freshest pastures feeds us,
   Turns our sighing into song.

Soon we pass this desert dreary,
   Soon we bid farewell to pain;
Never more be sad or weary,
   Never, never sin again.

HOW LONG!

Do they still linger—these slow-treading ages?
  How long must we still bear their cold delay?
Streak after streak the glowing dawn presages;
  And yet it breaks not—the expected day!

Each tossing year, with prophet-lip hath spoken,
  "Prepare your praises, earth awake and sing!"
And yet yon dome of blue remains unbroken;
  No tidings yet of the descending King!

Darkness still darkens; nearer now and nearer
    The lightnings gleam; the sea's scorched billows
      moan;
And the sere leaf of earth is growing serer;
  Creation droops, and heaves a bitterer groan.

O storm and earthquake, wind and warring thunder,
  Your hour is coming! One wild outburst more,
One other day of war, and wreck, and plunder;
  And then your desolating reign is o'er.

These plains are not your battle-field for ever;
   That glassy deep was never made for you;
These mountains were not built for you to shiver;
   These buds are not for your rude hands to strew.

Flee and give back to earth its verdant gladness,
   The early freshness of its unsoiled dew;
Take hence your sackcloth, with its stormy sadness;
   And let these wrinkled skies their youth renew.

Give back that day of days, the seventh and fairest,
   When, like a gem new-set, earth flung afar
Her glory, of creation's gems the rarest,
   Sparkling in beauty to each kindred star.

Come back, thou holy love, so rudely banished,
   When evil came, and hate, and fear, and wrong;
Return, thou joyous light, so quickly vanished;
   Revive, thou life that death has quenched so long

Re-fix, re-knit the chain so harshly broken,
   That bound this lower orb to yon bright heaven;
Hang out on high the ever-golden token,
   That tells of earth renewed and man forgiven.

Withdraw the veil that has for ages hidden
　　That upper kingdom from this nether sphere;
Renew the fellowship so long forbidden;
　　O God, thyself take up thy dwelling here!

A LITTLE WHILE.

BEYOND the smiling and the weeping
　　I shall be soon;
Beyond the waking and the sleeping,
Beyond the sowing and the reaping,
　　I shall be soon.
　　Love, rest, and home!
　　Sweet hope!
　　Lord, tarry not, but come.

Beyond the blooming and the fading,
　　I shall be soon;
Beyond the shining and the shading,
Beyond the hoping and the dreading,
　　I shall be soon.

Love, rest, and home !
Sweet hope !
Lord, tarry not, but come.

Beyond the rising and the setting
   I shall be soon ;
 Beyond the calming and the fretting,
Beyond remembering and forgetting,
   I shall be soon,
  Love, rest, and home !
  Sweet hope !
  Lord, tarry not, but come.

Beyond the gathering and the strowing
   I shall be soon ;
Beyond the ebbing and the flowing,
Beyond the coming and the going,
   I shall be soon.
  Love, rest, and home !
  Sweet hope !
  Lord, tarry not, but come.

Beyond the parting and the meeting
   I shall be soon.

Beyond the farewell and the greeting,
Beyond this pulse's fever-beating,
   I shall be soon.
   Love, rest, and home !
   Sweet hope !
   Lord, tarry not, but come.

Beyond the frost-chain and the fever
   I shall be soon ;
Beyond the rock-waste and the river,
Beyond the ever and the never,
   I shall be soon.
   Love, rest, and home !
   Sweet hope !
   Lord, tarry not, but come.

NOT VERY FAR.

SƆRELY, yon heaven, where angels see God's face,
  Is not so distant as we deem
From this low earth ?   'Tis but a little space,
  The narrow crossing of a slender stream ;
'Tis but a veil, which winds might blow aside :
Yes, these are all that us of earth divide,
From the bright dwelling of the glorified,—
  The Land of which I dream !

These peaks are nearer heaven than earth below,
  These hills are higher than they seem ;
'Tis not the clouds they touch, nor the soft brow
  Of the o'er-bending azure as we deem.
'Tis the blue floor of heaven that they up-bear ;
And like some old and wildly rugged stair,
They lift us to the land where all is fair,—
  The Land of which I dream !

These ocean-waves, in their unmeasured sweep,
  Are brighter, bluer, than they seem ;

True image here of the celestial deep,—
    Fed from the fulness of the unfailing **stream**,—
Heaven's glassy sea of everlasting rest,
With not a breath to stir its silent breast,
The sea that laves the land where all are blest,—
    The Land of which I dream !

And these keen stars, the bridal gems of **Night**,
    Are purer, lovelier, than they seem ;
Filled from the inner fountain of deep light,
    They pour down heaven's own beam ;
Clear-speaking from their throne of glorious **blue**,
In accents ever ancient, ever new,
Of the glad home above, beyond our view,—
    The Land of which I dream !

This life of ours, these lingering years of earth,
    Are briefer, swifter, than they seem ;
A little while, and the great second birth
    Of time shall come, the prophet's ancient theme !
Then He, the King, the Judge at length shall **come**,
And for this desert, where we sadly roam,
Shall give the kingdom for our endless home,—
    The Land of which I dream !

THE EVERLASTING MEMORIAL.

Up and away, like the dew of the morning,
   Soaring from earth to its home in the sun,—
So let me steal away, gently and lovingly,
   Only remembered by what I have done.

My name and my place and my tomb, all forgotten,
   The brief race of time well and patiently run,
So let me pass away, peacefully, silently,
   Only remembered by what I have done.

Gladly away from this toil would I hasten,
   Up to the crown that for me has been won;
Unthought of by man in rewards or in praises,—
   Only remembered by what I have done.

Up and away, like the odors of sunset,
   That sweeten the twilight as darkness comes on,—
So be my life,—a thing felt but not noticed,
   And I but remembered by what I have done.

Yes, like the fragrance that wanders in freshness,
  When the flowers that it came from are closed up
      and gone,—
So would I be to this world's weary dwellers,
  Only remembered by what I have done.

Needs there the praise of the love-written record,
  The name and the epitaph graved on the stone?
The things we have lived for,—let them be our story,
  We ourselves but remembered by what we have
      done.

I need not be missed, if my life has been bearing
  (As its summer and autumn moved silently on)
The bloom, and the fruit, and the seed of its season;
  I shall still be remembered by what I have done.

I need not be missed, if another succeed me,
  To reap down those fields which in spring I have
      sown;
He who ploughed and who sowed is not missed by
      the reaper,
  He is only remembered by what he has done.

Not myself, but the truth that in life I have spoken,
  Not myself, but the seed that in life I have sown,
Shall pass on to ages,—all about me forgotten,
  Save the truth I have spoken, the things I have
    done.

So let my living be, so be my dying;
  So let my name lie, unblazoned, unknown;
Unpraised and unmissed, I shall still be remembered;
  Yes,—but remembered by what I have done.

7

OUR ONE LIFE.

'Tis not for man to trifle ! Life is brief,
    And sin is here.
Our age is but the falling of a leaf,
    A dropping tear.
We have no time to sport away the hours,
All must be earnest in a world like ours.

Not *many* lives, but only *one* have we;—
    One, only one ;—
How sacred should that one life ever be—
    That narrow span !—
Day after day filled up with blessed toil,
Hour after hour still bringing in new spoil.

Our being is no shadow of thin air,
    No vacant dream,
No fable of the things that never were,
    But only seem.

'Tis full of meaning as of mystery,
Though strange and solemn may that meaning be.

Our sorrows are no phantom of the night,
    No idle tale;
No cloud that floats along a sky of light,
    On summer gale.
They are the true realities of earth,
Friends and companions even from our birth.

O life below—how brief, and poor, and sad!
    One heavy sigh.
O life above—how long, how fair, and glad;
    An endless joy.
Oh, to be done with daily dying here;
Oh, to begin the living in yon sphere!

O day of time, how dark! O sky and earth,
    How dull your hue;
O day of Christ—how bright! O sky and earth,
    Made fair and new!
Come, better Eden, with thy fresher green;
Come, brighter Salem, gladden all the scene!

THE CONSOLATION.

THE storm has broken, and the heavy blast,
    That stifled morn's free breath and shook its dew,
Is dying into sunshine ; and the last
    Dull cloud has vanished from yon arch of blue.

I know it is but for a day ; the war
    Must soon be waged again 'twixt earth and heaven ;
Another tempest will arise to mar
    The tranquil beauty of the fragrant even.

And yet I joy as storm on storm awakes ;—
    Not that I love the uproar or the gloom ;
But in each tempest over earth that breaks,
    I count one fewer outburst yet to come.

No groan creation heaves is heaved in vain,
    Nor e'er shall be repeated ; it is done.
Once heaved it never shall be heaved again ;
    Earth's pangs and throes are lessening one by one.

So falls the stroke of sorrow, and so springs
   Strange joy and comfort from the very grief,
Even to the weariest sufferer ; so brings
   Each heavy burden still its own relief.

One cross the less remains for me to bear ;
   Already borne is that of yesterday ;
That of to-day shall no to-morrow share ;
   To-morrow's, with itself, shall pass away.

That which is added to the troubled past
   Is taken from the future, whose sad store
Grows less and less each day, till soon the last
   Dull wave of woe shall break upon our shore.

The storm that yesterday ploughed up the sea
   Is buried now beneath its level blue ;
One storm the fewer now remains for me,
   Ere sky and earth are made for ever new.

THE REAL.

THERE are no dreams beyond the tomb!
  The night of dreams is o'er;
'Tis only here they go and come,
  On this dull, shadowy shore.

When we arise from off this restless couch
  Of weariness and pain,
When death awakes us with his stony touch
  Never to sleep again;

Then shadows vanish; the invisible
  Rises before our view;
On every side comes up the real,
  The certain, and the true.

And when the morn of morns shall come,
  The resurrection-day,
Then yet more real shall all become,
  And shadows pass away.

How true and great that world must be,
How false, how little this!
Man sees not what he seems to see,
He seems not what he is.

Here is the hollow and untrue;
This is the night of dreams;
Thickly o'erspread with mist and dew,
Earth is not what it seems.

Each morn is coming with its light,
To chase each shade and ill,
Then time's vain beauty shall take flight,
Like rainbow from the hill.

And truth returneth from on high;
Gone is the night of dreams,
Gone is the shadow and the lie,—
Earth shall be what it seems.

NOT HERE.

Softly the winds were fanning this fresh cheek,
  When heedless boyhood loved to dream and stray·
I loved earth's skies, nor deemed them sad or bleak:
  Its fields seemed still to breathe of joyous May.
I said, what better home shall this heart seek?
  Here let me dwell for aye.

Cold winter smote, frosts nipped, sore tempests broke,
  And the dark cloud shut out the beauteous day;
The fair flower perished, and the blast's rude shock
  Struck the strong pine, and swept its pride away;
My fond dream passed, I said, as I awoke.
  "I would not live alway."

Yet would I not turn back, nor faint, nor sigh,
  Nor shun the war, nor murmur at the doom;
I see the beacon-light of yonder sky
  Beyond the earth and sea—beyond the tomb!
And then I say, "O Saviour, ever nigh,
  Light me through this cold gloom"

NOT NOW.

Days come and go,
In joy or woe;
Days go and come,
In endless sum.
    Only the eternal day
       Shall come but never **go**
    Only the eternal tide
       Shall never ebb but flow.
    O long eternity,
    My soul goes forth to thee!

Suns set and rise
In these dull skies,
Suns rise and set,
Till men forget,
    The day is at the door,
    When they shall rise no more.
    O everlasting Sun,
    Whose race is never run,
    Be thou my endless light,
    Then shall I fear no night!

LIGHT'S TEACHINGS.

THE light is ever silent;
   It calls up voices over sea and earth.
   And fills the glowing air with harmonies,
   The lark's gay chant, the note of forest-dove,
   The lamb's quick bleat, and the bee's earnest hum,
   The sea-bird's winged wail upon the wave.
   It wakes the voice of childhood, soft and clear;
   The city's noisy rush, the village-stir,
   And the world's mighty murmur that had sunk,
   For a short hour, to sleep upon the down
   That darkness spread for wearied limbs and eyes.
   But still it sounds not, speaks not, whispers not!
   Not one faint throb of its vast pulse is heard
   By creature-ear.   How silent is the light!
   Even when of old it wakened Memnon's lyre,
   It breathed no music of its own; and still,
   When at sweet sunrise, on its golden wings,
   It brings the melodies of dawn to man,
   It scatters them in silence o'er the earth.

The light is ever silent;
    It sparkles on morn's million gems of dew,
    It flings itself into the shower of noon,
    It weaves its gold into the cloud of sunset—
    Yet not a sound is heard; it dashes full
    On yon broad rock, yet not an echo answers;
    It lights in myriad drops upon the flower,
    Yet not a blossom stirs, it does not move
    The slightest film of floating gossamer,
    Which the faint touch of insect's wing would shiver.

The light is ever silent;
    Most silent of all heavenly silences;
    Not even the darkness stiller, nor so still;
    Too swift for sound or speech, it rushes on
    Right through the yielding skies, a massive flood
    Of multitudinous beams; an endless sea,
    That flows but ebbs not, breaking on the shore
    Of this dark earth, with never-ceasing wave,
    Yet in its swiftest flow, or fullest spring-tide,
    Giving less sound than does one falling blossom,
    Which the May breeze lays lightly on the sward.

Such let my life be here;
    Not marked by noise but by success alone;

Not known by bustle but by useful deeds,
Quiet and gentle, clear and fair as light;
Yet full of its all-penetrating power,
Its silent but resistless influence;
Wasting no needless sound, yet ever working,
Hour after hour, upon a needy world.

Sunshine is ever calm;
There are no tempests in yon sea of beams,
That bright Pacific on whose peaceful bosom
All happy things come floating down to us.
Light has no hurricane, no angry blast,
No turbid torrent laying waste our plains.
Morn after morn goes by, and the fresh light,
Pours in upon the darkness, yet no storm
Awakes, no eddy stirs the tranquil glow;
No crested billow rises, and no foam
Drifting along, tells of some tumult past.

Sunshine is ever strong;
No blast can break or bend one single ray;
In seven-fold strength it faces wave and wind
Heedless of their opposing turbulence,
It passes through them in its quiet power,
Unruffled, and unbroken, and unbent.

No might of armies, and no rage of storms,
Can turn aside one sunbeam from its path,
Or bate its speed, or force it back again
To the far fountain-head from whence it came.

Sunshine is ever pure;
  No art of man can rob it of its beauty,
  Nor stain its unpolluted heavenliness.
  It is the fairest, purest thing in nature,
  Fit type of that fair heaven where all is pure,
  And into which no evil thing can enter,
  Where darkness comes not, where no shadow falls,
  Where night and sin can have no dwelling-place.

Sunshine is ever joyous;
  Its birthplace is in yon bright orb which flings,
  O'er cliff and vale its wealth of rosy smiles.
  Each sunbeam seems the very soul of joy;
  No sadness soils it; scattering gladsomeness,
  Like a bright angel, onward still it moves.
  The very churchyard brightens as the ray
  Alights upon its tombstones, and the turf
  Seems strangely heaving to the radiant glow,
  As if fore-dating the expected sunrise,
  When, at the first gleam of the Morning-Star

8

The faithful grave shall render up its treasure,
And sunshine, such as earth has never known,
Shall fill these skies with mirth, and smiles, and
    beauty
Erasing each sad wrinkle from their brow,
Which the long curse had deeply graven there.

EARTH'S BEAUTY.

WHERE the wave murmurs not,
Where the gust eddies not,
Where the stream rushes not,
Where the cliff shadows not,
Where the wood darkens not,
    I would not be!
Bright tho' the heavens were,
Rich tho' the flowers there,
Sweet tho' the fragrant air,
And all as Eden fair,
Yet as a dweller there,
    I would not be!
O wave, and breeze, and rill, and rock, and wood,
Was it not God himself that called you GOOD?

THE NIGHT AND THE MORNING.

To dream a troubled dream, and then awaken
    To the soft gladness of a summer sky;
To dream ourselves alone, unloved, forsaken,
    And then to wake 'mid smiles, and love, and joy;

To look at evening on the storm's rude motion,
    The cloudy tumult of the fretted deep;
And then at day-burst upon that same ocean,
    Soothed to the stillness of its stillest sleep—

So runs our course—so tells the church her story,
    So to the end shall it be ever told;
Brief shame on earth, but after shame the glory,
    That wanes not, dims not, never waxes old.

Lord Jesus, come, and end this troubled dreaming!
    Dark shadows vanish, rosy twilight break!
Morn of the true and real, burst forth, calm-beaming
    Day of the beautiful, arise, awake!

HOPE OF DAY.

Till the day dawn,
And the Day-star arise—
   Father, O keep thy son,
   Thy feeble, faithless one !
   O guide him through the waste,
   Till the long gloom be past.
   It is a night of fear ;
   The path is rough and drear;
   Clouds frown, blasts rush along,
   The tempests gather strong ;
   Strange perils compass me,
   Of flood, fire, rock, and sea ;
   Yet I, in loneliness,
   Would fain still onward press.
O felt and known, but yet unseen, be nigh ;
O loved and longed-for, hear each hidden sigh ;
Leave me not, struggling thus, to sink and die.

   Till the day dawn,
   And the Day-star arise—

O Saviour, let thy love,
Down dropping from above,
This withered soul renew
With thy flower-freshening dew !
O never-changing Friend,
My failing steps attend ;
Hold thou me up, and so
I shall pass safely through.
Still keep me at thy side,
Thou who for me hast died ;
O light me on my way,
My joy, my strength, my stay.
O clasp me closer to thy pierced side,
Thou who for me the death of deaths hast died ;
Let not this staggering faith be too too sorely tried.

Till the day dawn,
And the Day-star arise—
Spirit of gentle love,
Thou tempest-calming dove,
Come, and within me dwell,
Come, and all gloom dispel.
Most blessed Comforter,
My weary footsteps cheer.

O light and lamp divine,
Upon my midnight shine,
Better than star or moon,
Brighter than day's bright noon,
O let thy joyous ray
Turn all my night to day.
When thou art absent, even my joy is sad,
When thou art with me, even my grief is glad;
Let not thy silence now sorrow to sorrow add.

Till the day dawn,
And the Day-star arise—
Church of the living God,
Pursue thy upward road;
Look not behind nor stray
From the well-trodden way.
Be not ashamed to bear
Thy cross on earth, nor fear
Reproach and poverty,
For him who died for thee.
With girded loins press on,
Till the reward is won.
Think of thy absent Lord,
Hold fast thy plighted word.

Duff not thy weeds of widowhood, nor fear
To let the world, thro' which thou passest, hear
The widow's cry, and see the widow's faithful tear.

DAY-SPRING.

THE loving morn is springing
 From night's unloving gloom;
And earth seems now arising
 In beauty from the tomb,

See daylight far above us,
 Tinging each cloudy wreath,
Ere it showers itself in splendor
 Upon the plain beneath.

'T is sparkling on the mountain-peak,
 'T is hurrying down the vale,
'T is bursting thro' the forest-boughs,
 'T is freshening in the gale.

'T is mingling with the river's smile,
   'T is glistening in the dew,
'T is flinging far its silver net,
   O'er ocean's braided blue.

'T is blushing o'er the meadow's gold,
   'T is lighting on the flower,
Unfolding every gentle bud
   To the gladness of the hour.

'T is gilding the old ruin's moss,
   'T is gleaming from the spire ;
And thro' the crumbling window-shafts
   It shoots its living fire.

'T is quivering in the village smoke
   That curls the low roof o'er ;
It beats against the castle gate,
   And at the cottage door.

O'er the church-yard it is resting,—
   On stone, and grass, and mould,
Giving voice to each grey tombstone,
   As to Memnon's harp of old.

O the gay burst of beauty
   That is flushing over earth,
And calling forth its millions
   To holy morning mirth!

Yet look we for a sunrise
   More beautiful than this;
And watch we for a dawning
   Of purer light and bliss.

When a far fairer morning
   O'er greener hills shall rise.
And a far fresher sunlight
   Look down from bluer skies.

Is not creation weary?
   Has sin not reigned too long?
Hear, Lord, thy Church's pleading,
   Come, end her day of wrong!

DUST TO DUST.

Dust receive thy kindred !
   Earth take now thine own !
To thee this trust is rendered ;
   In thee this seed is sown.

Guard the precious treasure,
   Ever-faithful tomb !
Keep it all unrifled,
   Till the Master come.

Time's tide of change and uproar
   Breaks above thy head ;
Feet of restless millions
   O'er thy chambers tread.

Earthquakes, whirlwinds, tempests,
   Tear the quivering ground ;
Voices, trumpets, thunders,
   Fill the air around.

Roar of raging battle;
   Shout, and shriek, and wail,
Startle even the bravest,
   Turn the fresh cheek pale.

Torrent rolled on torrent,
   Bursts o'er bank and bar,—
Sweeping down our valleys,
   Swells the rising war.

Billow meeting billow,
   Beats the shattered strand,
Rousing ocean-echoes,
   Shaking sea and land.

But these sounds of terror
   Pierce not this low tomb;
Nor break the happy slumbers
   Of this quiet home.

Couch of the tranquil slumber
   For the weary brow;
Rest of the faint and toiling,
   Take this loved one now.

Turf of the shaded church-yard,
　　Warder of the clay,
Watch the toil-worn sleeper,
　　Till the awaking day.

Watch the well-loved sleeper,
　　Guard that placid form ;
Fold around it gently ;
　　Shield it from alarm.

Clasp it kindly, fondly,
　　To cherish, not destroy ;
Clasp it as the mother
　　Clasps her nestling joy.

Guard the precious treasure,
　　Ever faithful tomb ;
Keep it all unrifled
　　Till the Master come.

ARISE AND DEPART.

BRETHREN, arise,
  Let us go hence !
      Defiled, polluted thus,
      This is no home for us;
      Till earth is purified,
      We may not here abide.
      We were not born for earth,—
      The city of our birth,
      The better paradise,
      Is far above these skies.
      Upward then let us soar,
      Cleaving to dust no more !

Brethren, arise,
  Let us go hence !
      Death and the grave are here,
      The sick-bed and the bier.
      The children of the tomb
      May love this kindred gloom ;

But we, the deathless band,
Must see the deathless land.
The mortal here may rove,
The immortal dwell above.
Here we can only die,
Let us ascend on high !

Brethren, arise,
  Let us go hence !
    For we are weary here.
    The ever-falling tear,
    The ever-swelling sigh,
    The sorrow ever nigh,
    The sin still flowing on,
    Creation's ceaseless groan,
    The tumult near and far,
    The universal war,
    The sounds that never cease,—
    These are our weariness !

Brethren, arise,
  Let us go hence !
    This is not our abode ;
    Too far, too far from God !

The angels dwell not here ;
There falls not on the ear
The everlasting song,
From the celestial throng.
'Tis discord here alone,
Earth's melody is gone ,
Her harp lies broken now ;
Her praise has ceased to flow !

Brethren, arise,
Let us go hence !
The New Jerusalem,
Like a resplendent gem,
Sends down its heavenly light,
Attracting our dull sight.
I see the bright ones wait
At each fair pearly gate ;
I hear their voices call ;
I see the jasper wall,
The clear translucent gold,
The glory all untold !

Brethren, arise,
Let us go hence !

What are earth's joys and gems,
What are its diadems ?
Our crowns are waiting us
Within our Father's house.
Our friends above the skies
Are bidding us arise ;
Our Lord, he calls away
To scenes of sweeter day
Than this sad earth can know.
Let us arise and go !

THE KINGDOM.

PEACE ! earth's last battle has been won ;
   Its days of conflict now are o'er ;
The Prince of peace ascends the throne,
   And war has ceased from shore to shore.

Rest ! the world's day of toil is past ;
   Each storm is hushed above, below,
Creation's joy has come at last,
   After six thousand years of woe.

Messiah reigns ! earth's king has come !
   Its diadems are on his brow,
Its rebel kingdoms have become
   His everlasting kingdom now.

This earth again is Paradise ;
   The desert blossoms as the rose ;
Clothed in its robes of bridal bliss,
   Creation has forgot its woes.

O, long-expected, absent long,
   Star of creation's troubled gloom !
Let heaven and earth break forth in song,
   Messiah ! Saviour ! art thou come ?

For thou hast bought us with thy blood,
   And thou wast slain to set us free ;
Thou mad'st us kings and priests to God,
   And we shall reign on earth with thee !

9*

NEWLY FALLEN ASLEEP

PAST all pain for ever,
   Done with sickness now;
Let me close thine eyes, mother,
   Let me smooth thy brow.
Rest and health and gladness,—
   These thy portions now;
Let me press thy hand, mother,
   Let me kiss thy brow.

Eyes that shall never weep,
    Life's tears all shed,
    Its farewells said,—
These shall be thine!
    All well with thee;
O, would that they were mine!

A brow without a shade,
    Each wrinkle smoothed,
    Each throbbing soothed,

That shall be thine !
    All well with thee ;
O, would that it were mine !

A tongue that stammers not
    In tuneful praise,
    Through endless days,
That shall be thine !
    All well with thee.
O would that it were mine !

A voice that trembles not ;
    All quivering past,
    Death's sigh the last,—
That shall be thine !
    All well with thee ;
O, would that it were mine !

Limbs that shall never tire,
    Nor ask to rest,
    In service blest,—
These shall be thine !
    All well with thee ;
O, would that they were mine !

A frame that cannot ache;
   Earth's labors done,
   Life's battle won,—
That shall be thine!
   All well with thee;
O, would that it were mine!

A heart that flutters not;
   No timid throb,
   No quick-breathed sob,—
That shall be thine!
   All well with thee;
O, would that it were mine!

A will that swerveth not
   At frown or smile,
   At threat or wile,—
That shall be thine!
   All well with thee;
O, would that it were mine!

A soul still upward bent
   On higher flight,
   With wing of light,—

That shall be thine!
    All well with thee;
O, would that it were mine!

Hours without fret or care;
    The race well run,
    The prize well won,—
These shall be thine?
    All well with thee;
O, would that they were mine!

Days without toil or grief;
    Time's burdens borne
    With strength well-worn,—
These shall be thine
    All well with thee;
O, would that they were mine!

Rest without broken dreams,
    Or wakeful fears,
    Or hidden tears,
That shall be thine;
    All well with thee;
O, would that it were mine!

Life that shall fear no death,
God's life above,
Of light and love,—
That shall be thine!
All well with thee;
O, would that it were mine!

Morn that shall light the tomb,
And call from dust
The slumbering just,—
That shall be thine!
All well with thee
O, would that it were mine!

THE FLESH RESTING IN HOPE.

"The grave is mine house: I have made my bed in the
darkness .... the clods of the valley shall be sweet unto
him."—Job xxvii. 13, xi. 33

LIE down, frail body, here,
　Earth has no fairer bed,
No gentler pillow to afford,—
　Come, rest thy home-sick head.

Lie down, "vile body,"* here,
　This mould is smoothly strown,
No couch of flowers more softly spread,—
　Come, make this grave thine own.

Lie down with all thy aches,
　There is no aching here ;
How soon shall all thy life-long ills
　For ever disappear.

* Phil. iii. 21.

Thro' these well-guarded gates
　　No foe can entrance gain ;
No sickness wastes, nor once intrudes
　　The memory of pain.

The tossings of the night,
　　The frettings of the day,
All end, and like a cloud of dawn,
　　Melt from thy skies away.

Foot-sore and worn thou art,
　　Breathless with toil and fight,
How welcome now the long-sought sleep
　　Of this all-tranquil night.

Brief night and quiet couch
　　In some star-lighted room,
Watched but by one beloved eye,
　　Whose light dispels all gloom ;—

A sky without a cloud,
　　A sea without a wave,—
These are but shadows of thy rest.
　　In this thy peaceful grave.

Rest for the toiling hand,
   Rest for the thought-worn brow,
Rest for the weary way-sore feet,
   Rest from all labor now.

Rest for the fevered brain,
   Rest for the throbbing eye;
Thro' these parched lips of thine no more,
   Shall pass the moan or sigh.

Soon shall the trump of God
   Give out the welcome sound,
That shakes thy silent chamber-walls
   And breaks the turf-sealed ground.

Ye dwellers in the dust,
   Awake, come forth and sing;
Sharp has your frost of winter been,
   But bright shall be your spring.

'Twas sown in weakness here ;
   'Twill then be raised in power.
That which was sown an earthly seed,
   Shall rise a heavenly flower.

REST.

Not long, not long!—The spirit-wasting fever
    Of this strange life shall quit each throbbing vein;
And this wild pulse flow placidly for ever;
    And endless peace relieve the burning brain.

Earth's joys are but a dream; its destiny
    Is but decay and death. I's fairest form
Sunshine and shadow mixed. Its brightest·day
    A rainbow braided on the wreaths of storm.

Yet there is blessedness that changeth not;
    A rest with God, a life that cannot die;
A better portion and a brighter lot;
    A home with Christ, a heritage on high.

Hope for the hopeless, for the weary, rest,
    More gentle than the still repose of even!
Joy for the joyless, bliss for the unblest;
    Homes for the desolate in yonder heaven!

The tempest makes returning calm more dear ;
　　The darkest midnight makes the brightest star,
Even so to us when all is ended here,
　　Shall be the past, remembered from afar.

Then welcome change and death !   Since these alone
　　Can break life's fetters, and dissolve its spell ;
Welcome all present change, which speeds us on
　　So swift to that which is unchangeable.

A PILGRIM'S SONG.

A FEW more years shall roll,
　A few more seasons come ;
And we shall be with those that rest,
　Asleep within the tomb.
Then, O my Lord, prepare
　My soul for that great day ;
O wash me in thy precious blood,
　And take my sins away.

A few more suns shall set
　O'er these dark hills of time ;
And we shall be where suns are not,
　A far serener clime.
Then, O my Lord, prepare
　My soul for that blest day ;
O wash me in thy precious blood,
　And take my sins away.

A few more storms shall beat
　On this wild rocky shore ;

And we shall be where tempests cease,
And surges swell no more.
Then, O my Lord, prepare
My soul for that calm day;
O wash me in thy precious blood,
And take my sins away.

A few more struggles here,
A few more partings o'er,
A few more toils, a few more tears,
And we shall weep no more.
Then, O my Lord, prepare
My soul for that blest day;
O wash me in thy precious blood,
And take my sins away.

A few more Sabbaths here
Shall cheer us on our way;
And we shall reach the endless rest,
The eternal Sabbath-day.*

* The old Latin hymn expresses this well.
"Illic nec sabbato
Succedit sabbatum,
Perpes lætitia
Sabbatizantium.
10*

Then, O my Lord, prepare
　My soul for that sweet day ;
O wash me in thy precious blood,
　And take my sins away.

'Tis but a little while
　And He shall come again,
Who died that we might live, who lives
　That we with Him may reign.
Then, O my Lord, prepare
　My soul for that glad day ;
O wash me in thy precious blood,
　And take my sins away.

QUIS SEPARABIT

'Tis thus they press the hand and part,
   Thus have they bid farewell again;
Yet still they commune, heart with heart,
   Linked by a never-broken chain.

Still one in life and one in death,
   One in their hope of rest above;
One in their joy, their trust, their faith,
   One in each other's faithful love.

Yet must they part, and parting, weep;
   What else has earth for them in store?
These farewell pangs, how sharp and deep,
   These farewell words, how sad and sore!

Yet shall they meet again in peace,
   To sing the song of festal joy,
Where none shall bid their gladness cease,
   And none their fellowship destroy.

Where none shall beckon them away,
    Nor bid their festival be done ;*
Their meeting-time the eternal day,
    Their meeting-place the eternal throne.

There, hand in hand, firm linked at last,
    And, heart to heart, enfolded all,
They 'll smile upon the troubled past,
    And wonder why they wept at all.

Then let them press the hand and part,
    The dearly loved, the fondly loving,
Still, still in spirit and in heart,
    The undivided, unremoving.

* "Ibi festivitas sine fine."—Augustine.

FAR BETTER.

O SAFE at home, where the dark tempter roams not,
   How I have envied thy far happier lot!
Already resting where the evil comes not,
   The tear, the toil, the woe, the sin forgot.

O safe in port, where the rough billow breaks not,
   Where the wild sea-moan saddens thee no more;
Where the remorseless stroke of tempest shakes not;—
   When, when shall I too gain that tranquil shore?

O bright, amid the brightness all eternal,
   When shall I breathe with thee the purer air?—
Air of a land whose clime is ever vernal,
   A land without a serpent or a snare.

Away, above the scenes of guilt and folly,
   Beyond this desert's heat and dreariness,
Safe in the city of the ever-holy,
   Let me make haste to join thy earlier bliss.

Another battle fought, and oh, not lost—
  Tells of the ending of this fight and thrall,
Another ridge of time's lone moorland crossed,
  Gives nearer prospect of the jasper wall.

.Just gone within the veil, where I shall follow,
  Not far before me, hardly out of sight—
I down beneath thee in this cloudy hollow,
  And thou far up on yonder sunny height.

Gone to begin a new and happier story,
  Thy bitterer tale of earth now told and done;
These outer shadows for that inner glory
  Exchanged for ever.—O thrice blessed one!

O freed from fetters of this lonesome prison,
  How I shall greet thee in that day of days,
When He who died, yea rather who is risen,
  Shall these frail frames from dust and darkness
    raise.

WANDERING DOWN.

I AM wandering down life's shady path,
    ⁻Slowly, slowly, wandering down ;
I am wandering down life's rugged path,
    Slowly, slowly, wandering down.

Morn, with its store of buds and dew,
    Lies far behind me now ;
Morn, with its wealth of song and light,
    Lies far behind me now.

'T is the mellow flush of sunset now,
    'T is the shadow and the cloud ;
'T is the dimness of the dying eve,
    'T is the shadow and the cloud.

'T is the dreamy haze of twilight now,
    'T is the hour of silent trust ;
'T is the solemn hue of fading skies,
    'T is the time of tranquil trust.

The pleasant heights of breezy life,
  The pleasant heights are past;
The sunny slopes of buoyant life,
  The sunny slopes are past.

I shall rest in yon low valley soon,
  There to sleep my toil away;
I shall rest in yon sweet valley soon,
  There to sleep my tears away.

One little hour will soothe away
  Time's months of care and pain;
One quiet hour will dream away
  Time's years of care and pain.

Laid side by side with those I love,
  How calm that rest shall be!
Laid side by side with those I love,
  How soft that sleep shall be!

I shall rise and put on glory
  When the great morn shall dawn;
I shall rise and put on beauty
  When the glad morn shall dawn.

I shall mount to yon fair city,
  The dwelling of the blest;
I shall enter yon bright city,
  The palace of the blest.

I shall meet the many parted ones,
  In that one home of joy;
Lost love for ever found again,
  In that dear home of joy.

We have shared our earthly sorrow,
  Each with the other here;
We shall share our heavenly gladness,
  Each with the other there.

We have mingled tears together,
  We shall mingle smiles and song;
We have mingled sighs together,   .
  We shall mingle smiles and song.

11

THE ROD.

I WEEP, but do not yield,
　　I mourn, yet still rebel ;
My inmost soul seems steeled,
　　Cold and immovable.

The wound is sharp and deep ;
　　My spirit bleeds within ;
And yet I lie asleep,
　　And still I sin, I sin.

My bruised soul complains
　　Of stripes without, within ;
I feel these piercing pains—
　　Yet still I sin, I sin.

O'er me the low cloud hung
　　Its weight of shade and fear ;
Unmoved I passed along,
　　And still my sin is here.

You massive mountain-peak
　　The lightning rends at will;
The rock can melt or break—
　　I am unbroken still.

My sky was once noon-bright,
　　My day was calm the while,
I loved the pleasant light,
　　The sunshine's happy smile.

I said, my God, oh, sure,
　　This love will kindle mine;
Let but this calm endure,
　　Then all my heart is thine.

Alas, I knew it not!—
　　The summer flung its gold
Of sunshine o'er my lot,
　　And yet my heart was cold.

Trust me with prosperous days,
　　I said, O spare the rod;
Thee and thy love I 'll praise,
　　My gracious, patient God.

Must I be smitten, Lord ?
   Are gentler measures vaiu ?
Must I be smitten, Lord ?
   Can nothing save but pain ?

Thou trustedst me a while ;
   Alas ! I was deceived ;
I revelled in the smile,
   Yet to the dust I cleaved.

Then the fierce tempest broke,
   I knew from whom it came,
I read in that sharp stroke
   A father's hand and name.

And yet I did Thee wrong ;
   Dark thoughts of Thee came in, —
A froward, selfish throng—
   And I allowed the sin !

I did Thee wrong, my God,
   I wronged thy truth and love,
I fretted at the rod,
   Against thy power I strove.

I said, my God, at length,
    This stony heart remove,
Deny all other strength,
    But give me strength to love.

Come nearer, nearer still,
    Let not thy light depart;
Bend, break this stubborn will,
    Dissolve this iron heart.

Less wayward let me be,
    More pliable and mild;
In glad simplicity
    More like a trustful child.

Less, less, of self each day,
    And more, my God, of thee;
O keep me in the way,
    However rough it be.

Less of the flesh each day,
    Less of the world and sin;
More of thy Son I pray,
    More of Thyself within.

      11*

Riper and riper now,
　　Each hour let me become,
Less fit for scenes below,
　　More fit for such a home.

More moulded to Thy will,
　　Lord, let Thy servant be,
Higher and higher still,
　　Liker and liker thee.

Leave nought that is unmeet;
　　Of all that is mine own
Strip me; and so complete
　　My training for the throne.

STRENGTH BY THE WAY

Jesus, while this rough desert-soil
   I tread, be Thou my guide and stay ;
Nerve me for conflict and for toil ;
   Uphold me on my stranger-way.

Jesus, in heaviness and fear,
   'Mid cloud, and shade, and gloom I stray
For earth's last night is drawing near ;
   O cheer me on my stranger-way.

Jesus, in solitude and grief,
   When sun and stars withhold their ray,
Make haste, make haste to my relief ;
   O light me on my stranger-way.

Jesus, in weakness of this flesh,
   When Satan grasps me for his prey ;
O give me victory afresh ;
   And speed me on my stranger-way.

Jesus, my righteousness and strength,
  My more than life, my more than day ;
Bring, bring deliverance at length ;
  O come and end my stranger-way.

THE FEAST.

LOVE strong as death, nay stronger,
  Love mightier than the grave ;
Broad as the earth, and longer
  Than ocean's widest wave.
This is the love that sought us,
This is the love that bought us,
This is the love that brought us
  To gladdest day from saddest night,
  From deepest shame to glory bright,
  From depths of death to life's fair height,
  From darkness to the joy of light :
This is the love that leadeth
  Us to his table here,
This is the love that spreadeth
  For us this royal cheer.

THE STRANGER SEA-BIRD.

FAR from his breezy home of cliff and billow,
    Yon sea-bird folds his wing;
Upon the tremulous bough of this stream-shading
       willow
    He stays his wandering.

Fanned by fresh leaves, and soothed by blossoms
       closing,
    His lullaby the stream,
A stranger, in bewildered loneliness reposing,
    He dreams his ocean-dream :—

His dream of ocean-haunts, and ocean-brightness,
    The rock, the wave, the foam,
The blue above, beneath, the sea-cloud's trail of
       whiteness,
    His unforgotten home.

And he would fly, but cannot, for the shadows
    Of night have barred his way ;
How could he search a path across these woods and
      meadows
    To his far sea-home spray ?

Dark miles of thicket, swamp, and moorland dreary,
    Forbid his hopeless flight ;
With plumage soiled, eye dim, heart faint, and wing
      all weary,
    He waits for sun and light.

And I, in this far land, a timid stranger,
    Resting by Time's lone stream,
Lie dreaming, hour by hour, beset with night and
      danger,
    The Church's Patmos-dream :

The dream of home possessed, and all home's gladness,
    Beyond these unknown hills,
Of solace after earth's sore days of stranger-sadness,
    Beside the eternal rills.

Life's exile past, all told its broken story ;
  Night, death, and evil gone ;
This more than Egypt-shame exchanged for Canaan-
   glory,
  And the bright city won !

Come then, O Christ ! earth's Monarch and Redeemer,
  Thy glorious Eden bring,
Where I, even I, at last, no more a trembling dreamer,
  Shall fold my heavy wing.

HOPE DEFERRED.

How oft the morn has cheated us
   As with unsleeping eye,
We lay upon our silent couch,
   And watched the changing sky.

How often, as the heavy hours
   Stole by with endless haste,
We've said, Ah now the dawn begins,
   The weary night is past.

Hours went and came, but yet no streak
   On eastern cloud or hill,
We looked in vain, no sign appeared,
   'Twas night and silence still.

'Twas but the starlight, not the sun,
   The moonlight, not the day;
We thought it was the dawn, but now
   That dawn seems far away.

'Tis thus, beguiled with fond desire,
   And sick with hope deferred,
The watching Church, with eager ear,
   The well-known cry has heard :—

" He whom you look for is at hand,
   Both hope and fear are done !"
No, 'tis not yet,—and still she waits
   The still unrisen sun.

Age after age, in love and faith,
   She has with longing eye
Been watching every streak of dawn
   In yon perplexing sky.

And shall she now give up her trust,
   And turn her eye away,
As if there were no sun for her,
   No hope of light and day ?

She will not, for she knows how sure
   The promise of her Lord ;
She will not, for she knows how true
   Is the unchanging word.

12

The morn shall come ; nay He himself,
  Brighter than morn's best ray,
Shall come to bid the night depart,
  And bring at last the day.

Then shall the weary night-watch cease,
  When, counting each lone hour,
She marked the shadows flitting by
  The lattice of her tower.

'Twas not in vain she kept the watch
  When all around her slept ;
'Twas not in vain she waited thus,
  And loved, and longed, and wept.

It dawns at last, the long-loved morn,
  It comes, the meeting-day,
And in its joys shall be forgot
  The sorrows of delay.

THE BLANK.

One flower may fill another's place,
    With breath as sweet, with hues as glowing ;
One ripple in yon ocean-space
    Be lost amid another's flowing.

One star in yon bright azure dome
    May vanish from its sparkling cluster,
Unmissed, unmourned, and in its room
    Some rival orb eclipse its lustre.

But who shall fill a brother's room ?
    Or who shall soothe the bosom's grieving ?
Who heal the heart around his tomb
    Too faithfully, too fondly cleaving ?

Can I supply youth's memories ?
    Or speak the words in childhood spoken ?
Can I re-knit the severed ties ?
    Replace, retune the chord once broken ?

It is not here, it is not now,
　　That hearts are knit no more to sever;
Grief's wrinkles razed from cheek and brow,
　　And life's long blanks filled up for ever.

THE SLEEP OF THE BELOVED

"So he giveth his beloved sleep."—PSALM cxxvii. 2.

SUNLIGHT has vanished, and the weary earth
　　Lies resting from a long day's toil and pain,
And, looking for a new dawn's early birth,
　　Seeks strength in slumber for its toil again.

We too would rest; but ere we close the eye
　　Upon the consciousness of waking thought,
Would calmly turn it to yon star-bright sky,
　　And lift the soul to Him who slumbers not.

Above us is thy hand with tender care,
　　Distilling over us the dew of sleep:

Darkness seems loaded with oblivious air,
   In deep forgetfulness each sense to steep.

Thou hast provided midnight's hour of peace,
   Thou stretchest over us the wing of rest;
With more than all a parent's tenderness,
   Foldest us sleeping to thy gentle breast.

Grief flies away; care quits our easy couch,
   Till wakened by thy hand, when breaks the day—
Like the lone prophet by the angel's touch,—
   We rise to tread again our pilgrim-way.

God of our life! God of each day and night!
   Oh, keep us still till life's short race is run!
Until there dawns the long, long day of light,
   That knows no night, yet needs no star nor sun.

12*

THE LITTLE FLOCK.

A LITTLE flock! So calls He thee,
   Who bought thee with his blood ;
A little flock—disowned of men,
   But owned and loved of God.

A little flock! So calls He thee;
   Church of the first-born, hear!
Be not ashamed to own the name;
   It is no name of fear.

A little flock! Yes, even so ;
   A handful among men,
Such is the purpose of thy God ;
   So willeth He; Amen!

Not many rich or noble called,
   Not many great or wise ;
They whom God makes his kings and priests,
   Are poor in human eyes.

Church of the everlasting God,
  The Father's gracious choice,
Amid the voices of this earth
  How feeble is thy voice!

Thy words amid the words of earth,
  How noiseless and how low!
Amid the hurrying crowds of time,
  Thy steps how calm and slow!

But 'mid the wrinkled brows of earth
  Thy brow how free from care;
'Mid the flushed cheeks of riot here,
  Thy cheek how pale and fair!

Amid the restless eyes of earth,
  How steadfast is thine eye,
Fixed on the silent loveliness
  Of the far eastern sky.

A little flock! 'Tis well, 'tis well;
  Such be her lot and name;
Through ages past it has been so,
  And now 'tis still the same.

But the chief Shepherd comes at length
　　Her feeble days are o'er,
No more a handful in the earth,
　　A little flock no more.

No more a lily among thorns;
　　Weary, and faint, and few,
But countless as the stars of heaven,
　　Or as the early dew.

Then entering the eternal halls,
　　In robes of victory,
That mighty multitude shall keep
　　The joyous jubilee.

Unfading palms they bear aloft,
　　Unfaltering songs they sing;
Unending festival they keep,
　　In presence of the King.*

---

* Τῶν ἀγγέλων καὶ τῶν ἁγίων ἀει ἑορταζόντων.—ATHA-
NASIUS.

THE NAME OF NAMES.

Father, thy Son hath died
 The sinner's death of woe;
Stooping in love from heaven to earth,
 Our curse to undergo ;
 Our curse to undergo,
  Upon the hateful tree.
 Give glory to thy Son, O Lord,
 Put honor on that name of names
  By blessing me !

Father, thy Son hath borne
 The sinner's doom of shame;
Bearing his cross without the gate,
 He met the law's full claim ;
 He met the law's full claim,
  Sin's righteous penalty.
 Give glory to thy Son, O Lord,
 Put honor on that name of names
  By pardoning me !

Father, thy Son hath poured
　　His life-blood on this earth,
To cleanse away our guilt and stains,
　　To give us second birth ;
　　To give us second birth,
　　　From sin to set us free.
　　Give glory to thy Son, O Lord,
　　Put honor on that name of names
　　　By cleansing me !

Father, thy Son hath risen,
　　O'ercoming hell's dark powers ;
His surety-death was all for us,
　　His surety-life is ours ;
　　His surety-life is ours,
　　　Ours, ours eternally.
　　Give glory to thy Son, O Lord,
　　Put honor on that name of names
　　　By quickening me !

Father, thy Son to thee
　　Is now gone up on high,
Enthroned in heaven at thy right hand,
　　He reigns eternally ;
　　He reigns eternally,

In might and majesty.
Give glory to thy Son, O Lord.
Put honor on that name of names
By raising me !

Father, thy Son on earth,
 No one to own him found,
He passed among the sons of men
Rejected and disowned ;
Rejected and disowned,
That we received might be !
Give glory to thy Son, O Lord,
Put honor on that name of names
By owning me !

Father, thy Son is king,
Heaven's crown and earth's is his ;
For us, for us, he bought the crown,
For us he earned the bliss ;
For us he earned the bliss.
Amen, so let it be !
Give glory to thy Son, O Lord,
Put honor on that name of names
By crowning me !

MINE AND THINE.

"Didicisti quod nihil tui boni præcesserat, et gratiâ Dei conversus es ad Deum."—AUGUSTINE.

ALL that I *was*—my sin, my guilt,
　　My death was all my own;
All that I *am*, I owe to thee,
　　My gracious God alone.

The evil of my former state
　　Was mine and only mine;
The good in which I now rejoice
　　Is thine and only thine.

The darkness of my former state,
　　The bondage all was mine;
The light of life in which I walk,
　　The liberty is thine.

Thy grace first made me feel my sin,
 It taught me to believe;
Then, in believing peace I found,
 And now I live, I live.

All that I am, even here on earth,
 . All that I hope to be,
When Jesus comes and glory dawns,
 I owe it, Lord, to thee.

ABIDE IN HIM.

"Tecum volo vulnerari
 To libenter amplexari
  In cruce desidero."—OLD HYMN.

CLING to the Crucified!
 His death is life to thee,—
 Life for eternity.
 His pains thy pardon seal;
 His stripes thy bruises heal;
 His cross proclaims thy peace,
 . Bids every sorrow cease.

His blood is all to thee,
   It purges thee from sin;
It sets thy spirit free,
   It keeps thy conscience clean.
Cling to the Crucified!

Cling to the Crucified!
   His is a heart of love,
   Full as the hearts above;
   Its depths of sympathy
   Are all awake for thee:
   His countenance is light,
   Even to the darkest night.
   That love shall never change—
     That light shall ne'er grow dim;
   Charge thou thy faithless heart
     To find its all in him.
Cling to the Crucified!

THE BELOVED SON.

"This is my beloved Son, in whom I am well-pleased."—
ATT., iii. 17.

It is the Father's voice that cries
Mid the deep silence of the skies :
" This, this is my beloved Son,
In Him I joy, in Him alone.

"In Him my equal see revealed,
In Him all righteousness fulfilled,
In Him, the Lamb, the victim see,
Bound, bleeding, dying on the tree.

" And can you fail to love again ?
Far fairer he than sons of men !
His.very name is fragrance poured,
Immanuel, Jesus, Saviour, Lord !

"He died, and in his dying, proved
How much, how faithfully he loved;
At my right hand, his glories shine;
Is my beloved, sinner, *thine?*"

O full of glory, full of grace,
Redeemer of a ruined race,
Beloved of the Father, come,
Make in these sinful hearts a home!

Beloved of the Father, thou,
To whom the saints and angels bow;
Immanuel, Jesus, Saviour, come,
Make in these sinful hearts thy home!

THE SINBEARER.

"He was wounded for our transgressions; He was bruised for our iniquities."—ISA., iii. 5.

THY works, not mine, O Christ,
　　Speak gladness to this heart;
They tell me all is done;
　　They bid my fear depart.
　　　　　To whom save thee,
　　　　　　Who can alone
　　　　　　For sin atone,
　　　　Lord, shall I flee!

Thy pains, not mine, O Christ,
　　Upon the shameful tree,
Have paid the law's full price,
　　And purchased peace for me.
　　　　　To whom, save thee, etc.

13*

Thy tears, not mine, O Christ,
   Have wept my guilt away;
And turned this night of mine
   Into a blessed day.
          To whom, save thee, etc.

Thy bonds, not mine, O Christ,
   Unbind me of my chain,
And break my prison-doors,
   Ne'er to be barred again.
          To whom, save thee, etc.

Thy wounds, not mine, O Christ,
   Can heal my bruised soul;
Thy stripes, not mine, contain
   The balm that makes me whole.
          To whom, save thee, etc.

Thy blood, not mine, O Christ,
   Thy blood so freely spilt,
Can blanch my blackest stains
   And purge away my guilt.
          To whom, save thee, etc.

Thy cross, not mine, O Christ,
 Has borne the awful load
Of sins that none in heaven
 Or earth could bear but God.
   To whom, save thee, etc.

Thy death, not mine, O Christ,
 Has paid the ransom due ;
Ten thousand deaths like mine,
 Would have been all too few.
   To whom, save thee, etc

Thy righteousness, O Christ,
 Alone can cover me ;
No righteousness avails
 Save that which is of thee.
   To whom, save thee, etc.

Thy righteousness alone
 Can clothe and beautify ;
I wrap it round my soul ;
 In this I'll live and die.
   To whom, save thee, etc.

THE SUBSTITUTE.

> ' Jesu, plena caritate
>   Manus tuæ perforatæ
>   Laxent mea crimina;
>   Latus tuum lanceatum,
>   Caput spinis coronatum,
>   Hæc sint medicamina."—OLD HYMN.

I LAY my sins on Jesus,
    The spotless Lamb of God;
He bears them all and frees us
    From the accursed load.
I bring my guilt to Jesus,
    To wash my crimson stains
White in his blood most precious,
    Till not a stain remains.

I lay my wants on Jesus;
    All fulness dwells in Him.
He heals all my diseases,
    He doth my soul redeem.

I lay my griefs on Jesus,
 My burdens and my cares;
He from them all releases,
 He all my sorrows shares.

I rest my soul on Jesus,
 This weary soul of mine;
His right hand me embraces,
 I on his breast recline.
I love the name of Jesus,
 Immanuel, Christ, the Lord;
Like fragrance on the breezes,
 His name abroad is poured.

I long to be like Jesus,
 Meek, loving, lowly, mild,
I long to be like Jesus,
 The Father's holy child.
I long to be with Jesus
 Amid the heavenly throng,
To sing with saints his praises,
 To learn the angel's song.

LOST BUT FOUND.

"Arte mirâ, miro consilio,
  Quærens ovem suam summus opilio,
  Ut nos revocaret ab exilio."—OLD HYMN.

I WAS a wandering sheep,
  I did not love the fold ;
I did not love my Shepherd's voice,
  I would not be controlled.
I was a wayward child,
  I did not love my home,
I did not love my father's voice,
  I loved afar to roam.

The Shepherd sought his sheep,
  The Father sought his child,
They followed me o'er vale and hill,
  O'er deserts waste and wild.
They found me nigh to death,
  Famished, and faint, and lone ;

They bound me with the bands of love;
   They saved the wandering one!

They spoke in tender love,
   They raised my drooping head :
They gently closed my bleeding wounds,
   My fainting soul they fed.
They washed my filth away,
   They made me clean and fair ;
They brought me to my home in peace,—
   The long-sought wanderer !

Jesus my Shepherd is,
   'Twas He that loved my soul,
'Twas He that washed me in his blood,
   'Twas He that made me whole.
'Twas He that sought the lost,
   That found the wandering sheep,
'Twas He that brought me to the fold,
   'Tis He that still doth keep.

I was a wandering sheep,
   I would not be controlled :
But now I love my Shepherd's voice,
   I love, I love the fold !

I was a wayward child;
    I once preferred to roam,
But now I love my Father's voice,—
    I love, I love his home!

THE WORD MADE FLESH.

"Ye know the grace of our Lord Jesus Christ, that though
he was rich, yet for your sakes he became poor, that ye
through his poverty might be rich."—2 COR., viii. 9.

THE Son of God in mighty love,
    Came down to Bethlehem for me;
Forsook his throne of light above,
    An infant upon earth to be.

In love, the Father's sinless child
    Sojourned at Nazareth for me;
With sinners dwelt the undefiled,
    The Holy One in Galilee.

Jesus, whom angel-hosts adore,
    Became a man of griefs for me;
In love, though rich, becoming poor,
    That I through him enriched might be.

Though Lord of all, above, below,
 He went to Olivet for me;
There drank my cup of wrath and woe,
 When bleeding in Gethsemane.

The ever-blessed son of God
 Went up to Calvary for me;
There paid my debt, there bore my load,
 In his own body on the tree.

Jesus, whose dwelling is the skies,
 Went down into the grave for me;
There overcame my enemies,
 There won the glorious victory.

In love the whole dark path he trod,
 To consecrate a way for me;
Each bitter footstep marked with blood,
 From Bethlehem to Calvary.

'Tis finished all; the veil is rent,
 The welcome sure, the access free;—
Now then we leave our banishment,
 O Father, to return to thee!

14

THE DARKNESS AND THE LIGHT.

"Ye were sometime darkness, but now ye are light in the Lord."—Eph., v. 8.

"Let there be light," Jehovah said,
The beam awoke, the light obeyed ;
Bursting on chaos dark and wild,
Till the glad earth and ocean smiled.

Formless and void, and dark as night,
My heart remained, till heavenly light,
Obedient to the word divine,
On my dark soul began to shine.

Light broke upon my rayless tomb,
The day-star rose upon my gloom ;
And with its gentle new-born ray
Brightened my darkness into day.

Glory to Thee by all be given ;—
Of light the light, in earth and heaven ;
Of joys the joy, of suns the sun,
Jesus, the Father's chosen One.

THE VOICE FROM GALILEE.

"Of his fulness have all we received, and grace for grace."
—JOHN, i. 16.

I HEARD the voice of Jesus say,
    Come unto me and rest ;
Lay down, thou weary one, lay down
    Thy head upon my breast.
I came to Jesus as I was,
    Weary, and worn, and sad,
I found in Him a resting-place,
    And He has made me glad.

I heard the voice of Jesus say,
    Behold, I freely give
The living water,—thirsty one,
    Stoop down, and drink, and live.
I came to Jesus and I drank
    Of that life-giving stream,
My thirst was quenched, my soul revived,
    And now I live in Him.

I heard the voice of Jesus say,
  "I am this dark world's light,
Look unto me, thy morn shall rise
  And all thy day be bright.
I looked to Jesus and I found
  In Him, my Star, my Sun ;
And in that light of life I'll walk
  Till travelling days are done.

A BETHLEHEM HYMN.

"Mundum implens, in præsepio jacens."—AUGUSTINE.

He has come ! the Christ of God ;—
Left for us his glad abode ;
Stooping from his throne of bliss,
To this darksome wilderness.

He has come ! the Prince of Peace ;—
Come to bid our sorrows cease ;
Come to scatter, with his light,
All the shadows of our night.

He the mighty King has come !
Making this poor earth his home ·
Come to bear sin's sad load ;—
Son of David, Son of God.

He has come, whose name of grace
Speaks deliverance to our race ;
Left for us his glad abode ;
Son of Mary, Son of God !

Unto us a child is born !
Ne'er has earth beheld a morn
Among all the morns of time,
Half so glorious in its prime.

Unto us a Son is given !
He has come from God's own heaven ;
Bringing with him from above,
Holy peace and holy love.

14*

THIS DO IN REMEMBRANCE OF ME.

Here, O my Lord, I see thee face to face;
  Here would I touch and handle things unseen;
Here grasp with firmer hand the eternal grace,
  And all my weariness upon Thee lean.

Here would I feed upon the bread of God;
  Here drink with Thee the royal wine of heaven;
Here would I lay aside each earthly load,
  Here taste afresh the calm of sin forgiven.

This is the hour of banquet and of song,
  This is the heavenly table spread for me;
Here let me feast, and, feasting, still prolong
  The brief bright hour of fellowship with Thee.

Too soon we rise; the symbols disappear:
  The feast, though not the love, is passed and gone.
The bread and wine remove, but Thou art here,—
  Nearer than ever,—still my Shield and Sun.

I have no help but thine ; nor do I need
    Another arm save thine to lean upon.
It is enough, my Lord, enough, indeed ;
    My strength is in thy might,—thy might alone.

I have no wisdom, save in Him who is
    My Wisdom and my teacher, both in one ;
No wisdom can I lack while Thou art wise,
  • No teaching do I crave, save thine alone.

Mine is the sin, but thine the righteousness ;
    Mine is the guilt, but thine the cleansing blood ;
Here is my robe, my refuge, and my peace,—
    Thy blood, thy righteousness, O Lord my God.

I know that deadly evils compass me,
    Dark perils threaten, yet I would not fear,
Nor poorly shrink, nor feebly turn to flee,—
    Thou, O my Christ, art buckler, sword, and spear.

But see, the Pillar-cloud is rising now,
    And moving onward through the desert-night;
It beckons, and I follow, for I know
    It leads me to the heritage of light.

Feast after feast thus comes and passes by;
   Yet, passing, points to the glad feast above,
Giving sweet foretaste of the festal joy,
   The Lamb's great bridal feast of bliss and love.

CHRIST OUR PEACE.

I THOUGHT upon my sins, and I was sad,
   My soul was troubled sore and filled with pain;
But then I thought on Jesus and was glad,
   My heavy grief was turned to joy again.

I thought upon the law, the fiery law,
   Holy, and just, and good in its decree;
I looked to Jesus, and in Him I saw
   That law fulfilled, its curse endured for me.

I thought I saw an angry frowning God
   Sitting as Judge upon the great white throne;
My soul was overwhelmed,—then Jesus showed
   His gracious face, and all my dread was gone.

I saw my sad estate, condemned to die,
   Then terror seized my heart, and dark despair;
But when to Calvary I turned my eye,
   I saw the cross, and read forgiveness there.

I saw that I was lost, far gone astray,
   No hope of safe return there seemed to be;
But then I heard that Jesus was the way,
   A new and living way prepared for me.

Then in that way, so free, so safe, so sure,
   Sprinkled all o'er with reconciling blood,
Will I abide, and never wander more,
   Walking along in fellowship with God.

GOD'S ISRAEL.

" Happy sons of Israel,
    Who in pleasant Canaan dwell ;"
    Happy they, but happier we,
    If Jehovah's own we be.

Happy citizens who wait
    Within Salem's hallowed gate ;
    Happy they, but happier we
    Who the heavenly Salem see.

Happy sons of Levi there,
    Who within thy house of prayer
    Always stand ; but happier we,
    Day and night still praising Thee.

For Jerusalem above
    Is the city that we love ;
    Jerusalem our home we call,—
    Heavenly mother of us all.

The first two lines of the above are from the old translation
of the 66th Psalm by George Sandys.

THE SHADOW OF THE CROSS.

OPPRESSED with noon-day's scorching heat,
　　To yonder cross I flee ;　·
Beneath its shelter take my seat ;
　　No shade like this for me !

Beneath that cross clear waters burst,
　　A fountain sparkling free ;
And there I quench my desert thirst ;
　　No spring like this for me !

A stranger here, I pitch my tent
　　Beneath this spreading tree ;
Here shall my pilgrim life be spent ;
　　No home like this for me !

For burdened ones a resting-place,
　　Beside that cross I see ;
Here I cast off my weariness ;
　　No rest like this for me !

CHILD'S PRAYER.

" They that seek me early shall find me."—PROV., viii 17

HOLY FATHER! hear my cry,
   Holy Saviour! bend thine ear,
Holy Spirit! come thou nigh;
   Father, Saviour, Spirit, hear.

Father, save me from my sin,
   Saviour, I thy mercy crave,
Gracious Spirit, make me clean;
   Father, Son, and Spirit save.

Father, let me taste thy love,
   Saviour, fill my soul with peace,
Spirit, come my heart to move;
   Father, Son, and Spirit bless.

Father, Son, and Spirit—thou
   One Jehovah, shed abroad
All thy grace within me now;
   Be my Father and my God.

CHILD'S MORNING HYMN.

"He wakeneth morning by morning; he wakeneth mine ear to hear."—ISA., i. 4.

THE morning, the bright and the beautiful morning
   Is up, and the sunshine is all on the wing,
With its fresh flush of gladness the landscape adorn-
      ing,—
   A gladness which nothing but morning can bring.
The earth is awaking, the sky and the ocean,
   The river and forest, the mountain and plain;
The city is stirring its living commotion,
   And the pulse of the world is reviving again.

And we too awake, for our heavenly Father,
   Who soothed us so gently to sleep on his breast,
And made the soft stillness of evening to gather
   Around us, now calls us again from our rest.
But ere to our labors and duties returning,
   We hasten to give him the praise that is meet,
And in solemn devotion, the first hours of morning,
   Our freest and freshest, we lay at his feet.

15

Then, happy in heart, not a moment delaying,
    In the breeze of the dawning so pleasant and cool,
No loitering, no lingering, no trifling, no playing,
    But eager and active, we haste to the school.
How sweet are its hours that shine o'er us so brightly;
    How pleasant its lessons, how short seems the day;
Its hours are but moments, they fly off so lightly,
    When we are so busy, so cheerful, and gay.

Then away to the school in the sweet summer morn-
      ing,
    God's blessing upon us, his light on our road;
And let all the lessons we daily are learning,
    Be only to bring us more surely to God.
O now, let us haste to our heavenly Father,
    And ere the fair skies of life's dawning be dim,
Let us come with glad hearts, let us come altogether,
    And the morn of our youth let us hallow to Him.

TO M. L. B.

No night descend on thee :
   O'er thee no shadows come !
Safe be thy journey through
   This vale of cloud and gloom.

Daybreak be ever thine ;
   With fresh and rosy hours,
Calm sunshine of the morn,
   Odors, and dews, and flowers.

Light dwell in thee, and thou
   Dwell ever in the light ;
No wrinkle on thy brow,
   Thine eye still blue and bright.

One long sweet spring be thine,
   With buds still bursting through,
Fresh blossoms every hour,
   And verdure fair and new.

Peace be thy gentle guest,
Peace holy and divine ;
God's blessed sunlight still,
Upon thy pathway shine.

His Spirit fill thy soul,
And cast out every sin,
His own deep joy impart,
And make a heaven within.

THE TWO ERAS OF THE LAND.

Of old they sung the song of liberty,
  They sung it upon mountain and on plain,
Till every echo of both land and sea
  Pealed back the song again.

They poured it on the morning's genial gale,
  It floated out upon the evening's calm,
And the rich stream-breeze from each fragrant vale
  Gave back the song in balm.

The peasant sang it in his straw-roofed cot,
  The noble sang it in his princely hall,
Till the vexed land, responding to the note,
  Rose up at freedom's call.

The blithe blue morning's newly-wakened ray
  Of cloudless summer coming freshly down,
Saw chains and bondage, tears and slavery,
  The tyrant's sword and frown.

15*

The northern noonday saw the rising war,
    Like sudden tempest on a wind-swept sea,
The shout rose upwards to the evening-star,
    The land, the land is free !

Amid the oppressor's threats they planted high
    The ancient flag of liberty,
That banner floats unthreatened to the sky,—
    The Bruce hath set them free !

They sung the song of liberty again,
    'Twas a still louder song than that of yore ;
It went like thunder-notes o'er hill and plain,
    It woke each echoing shore.

It woke the heart of age and heedless youth,
    It woke the spirit of the sleeping land,
It roused them to the voice of holy truth ;
    Who could that voice withstand ?

Hear ye the truth, and hearing it, obey ;
    Know ye the truth, the truth shall make you free ;
Love not the midnight, love the lightsome day,
    That light is life and liberty.

The Free One makes you free ; he breaks the rod,
 He bids you lift your heads to sky and sun,
As freemen of the everlasting God,
 Kneeling to Him alone.

The Free One makes you free ; be slaves to none,
 Priest, prince, or self, in body or in soul ;
Serve thou with all thy strength thy God alone,
 Yield but to His control.

The True One gives you truth ; a heritage,
 Richer than that which kings may buy or sell,
For children's children to the farthest age ;
 Guard thou that treasure well.

Round went the message, over rock and plain,
 Like burning words from lips of prophet old,
Priest, king, and lord opposed the voice in vain,
 It would not be controlled.

Wide o'er the land went forth the new born day,
 Brightening alike the cot, the hall, the throne,
Long years of darkness vanish at its ray,
 Ages of night have gone.

The Christ has come, the breaker of all chains,
    The giver of the heavenly liberty;
Peace, light, and freedom to these hills and plains!—
    The land, the land is free!

MARTYR'S HYMN.

"The glory of children are their fathers."—PROV., xvii. 6.

THERE was gladness in Zion, her standard was flying
    Free o'er her battlements, glorious and gay;
All fair as the morning shone forth her adorning,
    And fearful to foes was her godly array.

There is mourning in Zion, her standard is lying
    Defiled in the dust, to the spoiler a prey;
And now there is wailing, and sorrow prevailing,
    For the best of her children are weeded away.

The good have been taken, their place is forsaken;
    The man and the maiden, the green and the grey
The voice of the weepers wail over the sleepers,
    The martyrs of Scotland that now are away!

The hue of her waters is crimsoned with slaughters,
   The blood of the martyrs has reddened the clay ;
And dark desolation broods over the nation,
   For the faithful are perished, the good are away !

On the mountains of heather they slumber together ;
   On the wastes of the moorland their bodies decay ;
How sound is their sleeping, how safe is their keeping,
   Though far from their kindred they moulder away.

Their blessing shall hover, their children to cover,
   Like the cloud of the desert, by night and by day,
Oh, never to perish, their names let us cherish,
   The martyrs of Scotland that now are away !

SURSUM CORDA.

Go up, go up, my heart,
   Dwell with thy God above ;
For here thou canst not rest,
   Nor here give out thy love.

Go up, go up, my heart,
   Be not a trifler here ;
Ascend above these clouds,
   Dwell in a higher sphere.

Let not thy love flow out
   To things so soiled and dim ,
Go up to heaven and God,
   Take up thy love to him.

Waste not thy precious stores
   On creature-love below ;
To God that wealth belongs,
   On him that wealth bestow.

Go up, reluctant heart,
　　Take up thy rest above ;
Arise, earth-clinging thoughts,
　　Ascend, my lingering love !

THE REST-DAY.

Hæc dies, in quâ quies
　　Mundo redditur ;
　　Tempus enim est,
Quo resurrexit, qui nos dilexit.

Gaude, plaude, ama, clama
　　Voce validâ,
　　Surge, curre,
Vere quære Christum istum,
Corde sorde procul positâ.—OLD HYMN.

For thee we long and pray,
　　O blessed Sabbath-morn !
And all the week we say,
　　O ! when wilt thou return ?
　　　　Come, come away,
　　　　　Day of glad rest,
　　　　　Of days the best,
　　　　Sweet Sabbath-day !

Thou tellest us how Christ
  Arose and left the tomb;
And all the week we say,
  O! when will Sabbath come?
    Come, come away, etc.

Thou tellest us how we,
  Like him shall leave the tomb;
And all the week we say,
  O! when will Sabbath come?
    Come, come away, etc.

Thou tellest of a rest,
  A peaceful happy home,
Where all the saints are blest;
  O! when will Sabbath come?
    Come, come away, etc.

THE INNER CALM.

Calm me, my God, and keep me calm,
   While these hot breezes blow,
Be like the night-dew's cooling balm
   Upon earth's fevered brow.

Calm me, my God, and keep me calm,
   Soft resting on thy breast,
Soothe me with holy hymn and psalm
   And bid my spirit rest.

Calm me, my God, and keep me calm,
   Let thine outstretched wing
Be like the shade of Elim's palm,
   Beside her desert spring.

Yes, keep me calm, though loud and rude
   The sounds my ear that greet
Calm in the closet's solitude,
   Calm in the bustling street.

Calm in the hour of buoyant health,
　Calm in my hour of pain,
Calm in my poverty or wealth,
　Calm in my loss or gain.

Calm in the sufferance of wrong,
　Like Him who bore my shame,
Calm 'mid the threatening, taunting throng,
　Who hate thy holy name.

Calm when the great world's news with power
　My listening spirit stir;
Let not the tidings of the hour
　E'er find too fond an ear.

Calm as the ray of sun or star
　Which storms assail in vain,
Moving unruffled through earth's war,
　The eternal calm to gain.

THE DISBURDENING

Lay down thy burden here;
  With such a weary load
Thou canst not climb yon hill,
  Yon steep and rugged road.

'Tis rough, and wild, and high,
  Thickets and rocks impede;
Scant resting-place between,
  How canst thou upward speed!

Lay down thy burden here,
  Poor weary son of time;
So shall thy limbs be strong,—
  So shalt thou upward climb.

The sun is hot, no cloud
  To shield thee from his ray;
It scorches up thy strength,
  Stay now, poor climber, stay.

Thou breathest hard, the drops
   Are on thy burning brow;
Try not another step,
   Lay down thy burden now.

So shalt thou climb yon hill,
   Up to its steepest height;
Like eagle of the rock,
   With easy joyful flight.

So shalt thou bear the toils
   Thy God appoints to thee;
So shalt thou serve thy God
   In happy liberty.

COMPANIONSHIP.

Not with the light and vain,
   The man of idle feet and wanton eyes;
Not with the world's gay, ever-smiling train;
   My lot be with the grave and wise.

Not with the trifler gay,
   To whom life seems but sunshine on the wave,
Not with the empty idler of the day;
   My lot be with the wise and grave.

Not with the jesting fool,
   Who knows not what to sober truth is due,
Whose words fly out without or aim or rule!
   My lot be with the wise and true.

Not with the man of dreams,
   In whose bright words no truth nor wisdom lies,
Dazzling the fervent youth with mystic gleams;
   My lot be with the simply wise.

16*

With them I'd walk each day,
    From them time's solemn lessons would I learn;
That false from true, and true from false I may
    Each hour more patiently discern.

THE HEAVENLY SOWING.

Sower divine!
    Sow the good seed in me,
    Seed for eternity.
    'Tis a rough barren soil,
    Yet by thy care and toil,
    Make it a fruitful field
    An hundred fold to yield.
Sower divine,
Plough up this heart of mine!

Sower divine!
    Quit not this wretched field
    Till thou hast made it yield;
    Sow thou by day and night,
    In darkness and in light.

Stay not thy hand, but sow;
Then shall the harvest grow.
Sower divine,
Sow deep this heart of mine!

Sower divine!
  Let not this barren clay
  Lead thee to turn away;
  Let not my fruitlessness
  Provoke thee not to bless;
  Let not this field be dry,
  Refresh it from on high.
Sower divine,
Water this heart of mine!

DISAPPOINTMENT.

"Ecce mundus turbat et amatur, quid si tranquillus esset."
--AUGUSTINE.

TRUST not these seas again,
   Tho' smooth and fair;
Trust not these waves again,
   Shipwreck is there.

Trust not these stars again,
   Tho' bright and fair;
Trust not these skies again,
   Tempest is there.

Trust not that breeze again,
   Gentle and fair;
Trust not these clouds again,
   Lightning is there.

Trust not that isle again,
   Flower-crowned and fair;
Trust not its rocks again,
   Earthquake is there.

Trust not these flowers again,
　　Fragrant and fair ;
Trust not that rose again,
　　Blighting is there.

Trust not that earth again,
　　Verdant and fair ;
Trust not its fields again,
　　Winter is there.

Trust not these hopes again,
　　Sunny and fair ;
Trust not that smile again,
　　Peril is there.

Trust not this world again,
　　Smiling and fair ;
Trust not its sweets again,
　　Wormwood is there.

Trust not its love again,
　　Sparkling and fair ;
Trust not its joy again,
　　Sorrow is there.

THE TIME TO MEET,

'T is autumn now;
    And as we part,
    The dry brown leaf
    Is rustling o'er the ground;
Making the sadness sadder, and the cloud
Of the long farewell deeper in its gloom.

Not thus let us meet;
    Mid falling leaves
    And sere, frost-stricken flowers;
    But when the leaf is budding in its freshness,
    And the rich blossom putting forth its gladness.
Not thus let us meet;
    It is too sad;
    But when the buried verdure
    Is coming up to meet the joyous sun,
    When the new spring looks round upon the hills,
    Full of youth's buoyant promise and bright song,
Then let us meet.

Yes, when the spring-breeze blows,
And the gay garden blooms,
And the wide forest waves with budding green,
And the freed streamlet warbles through the broom,
And the clear air takes up the happy note
Of skylark singing to the rosy dawn,
    Then let us meet ;
And meeting, cheer each other's weary heart
With the dear hope of everlasting spring,
And the fair land that spreads beneath the slopes
    Of the eternal hills,
    Where nothing dies ;
    Where nothing fades ;
But all is without ending or decay,
    The sky, the sun, the light,
    The peace, the truth, the love,
And above all, the joy !

GONE BEFORE.

THOU art in heaven, and I am still on earth;
'Tis years, long years, since we were parted here,
I still a wanderer amid grief and fear,
And thou the tenant of a brighter sphere.
 Yet still thou seemest near;
 But yesterday it seems,
 Since the last clasp was given,
 Since our lips met,
 And our eyes looked into each other's depths.

Thou art amid the deathless, I still here,
Amid things mortal, in a land of graves,
A land o'er which the heavy-beating waves
Of changing time move on, a land where raves
 The storm, which whoso braves
 Must have his anchor fixed
 Firmly within the vail;—
 So let my anchor be;
 Such be my consolation and my hope!

Thou art amid the sorrowless, I here
Amid the sorrowing; and yet not long
Shall I remain 'mid sin, and fear, and wrong:
Soon shall I join you in your sinless song.

Thy day has come, not gone,
Thy sun has risen, not set,
Thy life is now beyond
The reach of death or change;
Not ended but begun,
Such shall our life be soon,
And then,—the meeting-day,
How full of light and joy!
All fear of change cast out,
All shadows passed away,
The union sealed for ever
Between us and our Lord.

17

THE ELDER BROTHER.

Yes, for me, for me he careth
    With a brother's tender care;
Yes, with me, with me he shareth
    Every burden, every fear.

Yes, o'er me, o'er me he watcheth,
    Ceaseless watcheth, night and day:
Yes, even me, even me he snatcheth
    From the perils of the way.

Yes, for me he standeth pleading,
    At the mercy-seat above;
Ever for me interceding,
    Constant in untiring love.

Yes, in me abroad he sheddeth
    Joys unearthly,—love and light;
And to cover me he spreadeth
    His paternal wing of might.

Yes, in me, in me he dwelleth;—
   I in him, and he in me!
And my empty soul he filleth,
   Here and through eternity.

Thus I wait for his returning,
   Singing all the way to heaven;
Such the joyful song of morning,
   Such the tranquil song of even.

LIFE FROM THE DEAD

Spirit of everlasting grace,
　Infinite source of life, come down,
These tombs unlock, these dead upraise,
　Thy glorious power and love make known.

Breathe o'er this valley of the dead,
　Send forth thy quickening might abroad,
Till, rising from their tombs, they spread,
　In full array,—the host of God !

Thy heritage lies desolate,
　And all thy pleasant places mourn ;
O look upon our low estate,
　In loving kindness, Lord, return !

Now let thy glory be revealed,
　Now let thy presence with us rest ;—
O heal us, and we shall be healed !
　O bless us, and we shall be blest !

EVER NEAR.

I CLOSE my heavy eye,—
    Saviour ever near!
I lift my soul on high
    Through the darkness drear.
Be thou my light, I cry,
    Saviour ever dear!

I feel thine arms around,
    Saviour, ever near!
With thee let me be found,
    So shall I never fear,
Whatever ill abounds ;—
    Saviour, ever dear!

Thine is the day and night,
    Saviour, ever near ;
Thine is the dark and light,—
    Be thou my covert here ;
O shield me with thy might,
    Saviour, ever dear!

17*

And when I come to die,
    Saviour, ever near,
Receive my parting sigh :
    And, in the hour of fear,
Be to my spirit nigh,
    Saviour, ever dear !

IT IS FINISHED.

BLESSED be God, our God !
  Who gave for us his well-beloved Son,
  His gift of gifts, all other gifts in one.
Blessed be God, our God !

What will he not bestow ?
  Who freely gave this mighty gift, unbought,
  Unmerited, unheeded and unsought,
What will he not bestow ?

He spared not His Son !
  'Tis this that silences each rising fear,
  'Tis this that bids the hard thought disappear
He spared not His Son !

Who shall condemn us now?
　　Since Christ has died, and risen, and gone above,
　　For us to plead at the right hand of love,
Who shall condemn us now?

'Tis God that justifies!
　　Who shall recall the pardon or the grace,
　　Or who the broken chain of guilt replace?
'Tis God that justifies!

The victory is ours!
　　For us in might came forth the One,
　　For us he fought the fight, the triumph won;
The victory is ours!

PRESS ON.

Be brave, my brother!
  Fight the good fight of faith
    With weapons proved and true;
  Be faithful and unshrinking to the death,
    Thy God will bear thee through;
  The strife is terrible,
    Yet 'tis not, 'tis not long;
  The foe is not invincible,
    Though fierce and strong.

Be brave, my brother!
  The recompense is great,
    The kingdom bright and fair;
  Beyond the glory of all earthly state,
    Shall be the glory there.
  Grudge not the heavy cost,
    Faint not at labor here,
  'Tis but a life-time at the most,
    The day of rest is near.

Be brave, my brother!
  He, whom thou servest, slights
    Not even his weakest one;
  No deed, though poor, shall be forgot,
    However feebly done.
  • The prayer, the wish, the thought,
    The faintly spoken word,
  The plan that seemed to come to nought,
    Each has its own reward.

Be brave, my brother!
  Enlarge thy heart and soul;
    Spread out thy free glad love,
  Encompass earth, embrace the sea,
    As does that sky above.
  Let no man see thee stand
    In slothful idleness,
  As if there were no work for thee
    In such a wilderness.

Be brave, my brother!
  Stint not the liberal hand,
    Give in the joy of love;
  So shall thy crown be bright, and great
    Thy recompense above;

Reward,—not like the deed,
   That poor weak deed of thine ;
But like the God himself who gives,
   Eternal and divine.

LAUS DEO.

EVERLASTING praises
   To the Father be !
Everlasting praises
   To the Saviour be !
Everlasting praises
   To the Spirit be !
Everlasting praises
   To the blessed Trinity !

Everlasting praises
   For the Father's love !
Everlasting praises
   For the Saviour's love !
Everlasting praises
   For the Spirit's love !
Everlasting praises
   To the Three-One God of love !

CREATION.

In the beginning was the THE WORD;
      The Word was God.
In the beginning was the Word;
        And His abode
        From everlasting was with God.
          His name
          I AM,—
        Jehovah, God, the Lord.
        Ever to be adored;
      The eternal Son,—
      The ever-blessed One.
From all, to all eternity,
The brightness of the eternal Father's glory He!

Creator of the heaven and earth,
      Their Lord and King.
Creator of the heaven and earth,
      The angels sing!

To him all praise and glory bring;
His power
Adore,
From which all things had birth,
By which they still stand forth
In beauty glad,
With heavenly radiance clad.
Praise, praise His ever-flowing love,
That brightens all below, and gladdens all above.

"Let there be light," 'twas He that spoke,
"And there was light."
"Let there be light," 'twas He that spoke,
And the long night
At His divine command took flight.
The ray
Of day
O'er the deep darkness broke;
The sleeping world awoke:
Earth, sea, and sky
Burst forth in praises high
To Him who made the light to be:
He is the Light of light, and there is none but He!

This green, glad, goodly earth of ours
      His hand did frame.
This green, glad, goodly earth of ours
      Doth still proclaim,
      By day and night, His wondrous name.
        These seas
        Are His;
      Each mountain-peak that towers;
      These clouds with their fresh showers;
    These streams that run
    Quick-glancing in the sun,
These tossing woods, these trembling flowers,
And all that men call bright in this bright world of
    ours.

All that has life and breath He made,
      In earth, sea, sky.
All that has life and breath He made,
      To swim or fly,
    To creep or bound; and, in his eye,
      All good
      They stood,
    In beauty pure arrayed,
    As if they could not fade.

18

How fair this frame,
How excellent His name,
Who, in the fulness of His love,
Transplanted thus to earth the Paradise above !

All glory to the eternal WORD,
  Earth's Lord and King :
All glory to the eternal Word,
  Ye angels, sing.
  Ye sons of earth your tribute bring :
  His name,
  Proclaim,—
  Jehovah, God, the Lord ;
  Ever to be adored.
 Maker of all,
 Before him prostrate fall :
By every voice, and tribe, and tongue,
For ever and for ever be His praises sung.

DESERT LILIES.

Desert lilies, desert lilies !
   Blooming gaily in the sand
   Of this untrodden land ;
      With your leaf as soft and green,
      With your flower as fair in tint,
      As delicate in form
      As beautiful in hue,
      As fragrant and as fresh,
      As sweet at morn or even,
      As bright with smiles and dew,
   As in our happier plains
   Cherished by genial rains.

Desert lilies, desert lilies !
   Shining quietly like gems,
   Upon your verdant stems ;
      With no breath of man to dim you,
      With no city smoke to taint you,
      With no hand of man to pluck you,

With no eye of man to see you,
With no care of man to tend you,
With no child's glad face to watch you,
As you spring and as you bloom;
With no sorrowing lip to mourn you,
As you fade and as you die.
Nought but the wind's caress
In this lone wilderness!

Desert lilies, desert lilies!
Bidding welcome to the ray
Of this fierce-flaming day,
Courting no cloud, nor shade
Of rock, or cliff, or glade,
Opening your purple eyes
Unfearing to these skies.
What sunlight ye have seen,
What moonshine in these heavens,
What starlight clear and glad,
What soft dew at early dawn,
What cool breezes o'er this waste!
What sunsets ye have seen,
On these wondrous peaks around,
What tints of purple glow.

At sunset or at morn ?
What strange and solemn airs
Have ye heard, as all night long
Ye listened, night by night,
Coming forth from you wild crags,
Moving out along these slopes,
Stealing down yon mighty hill
To the silent sands beneath,
Creeping through the wiry boughs,
Of these tarfas far and near.
O life, how glad and blest,
Thou seem'st in such a waste !
O beauty, what a power,
To cheer in loneliest hour !
O earth where is the spot,
Which thy God visits not?
On which his eye of light
Rests not in gentle love ;
O'er its most barren sands,
Rejoicing from above !
O desert rocks, if one small leaf
Can make these wastes look fair,
What will ye be when these scorched plains,
Earth's richest buds shall bear ?

18*

When eastern suns shall cease to scorch
 And storms no more destroy ;
And these lone valleys shall give forth
 Their streams, and flowers, and **joy.**

SUMMER GLADNESS.

WHAT a world with all its sorrows !
 What a scene, would it but stay ;
What an earth, if all its morrows
 Were as fair as this " to-day !"

When earth's summer pulse is beating
 With the fever-fire of June,
And the flowers fling up their greeting,
 Quivering to the joyous noon.

When the streamlet, smiling gladly,
 Hurries calmly, brightly by,
Not a voice around speaks sadly,
 Not a murmur nor a sigh.

Sunbeams with their fond caresses,
   . Smooth each rosebud's velvet fold,
Lingering in the glowing tresses
   Of yon rich laburnum's gold.

Nature all its gay adorning
   Opens to the day's bright bliss,
Like a child at early morning,
   Wakened by its mother's kiss.

What a world ! when all its sorrow
   Shall for ever pass away !
What an earth ! when each " to-morrow"
   Shall be fairer than " to-day."

THE FRIEND.

There is a star in yonder sky,
   Above all stars it seems to shine,
'Tis long since first it fixed my eye,
   And I have learned to call it mine.

It rose out of my own blue sea,
   Then passed above those mountains green,
Moving all placidly,
   As if it loved to watch the scene.

Far up the heavens it floated slow,
   Gleaming across yon solemn tower,
As if it loved the scene below ;—
   A willing lingerer hour by hour.

It seemed to take its place each night,
   As sentinel to guard my rest,
An eye of love and gentle light,
   Pouring sweet thoughts into my breast.

In through my lattice as I lay
   Half soothed to sleep, it nightly shone,
And as I gazed upon its ray
   I felt that I was not alone.

What tears that gentle star has dried,
   What joy that sparkling orb has given ;
Thoughts for this earth too high, too wide,
   Dreams of its own all-radiant heaven.

It spoke of day beyond this night,
   In the glad land where all is fair ;
It pointed to the home of light,
   And bid me rest my spirit there.

It spoke of Him whose love is light,
   Whose death is life, whose cross is peace,
Whose favor is the star of night,
   The source and pledge of endless bliss.

May I not love that star on high ?
   May not its light the fairest seem ?
May I not trace a loving eye,
   A kindly smile in every beam ?

THE BLANK.

The flowers of Spring have come and gone;
  Bright were the blossoms, brief their stay;
They shone, and they were shone upon,
  They flourished, faded, passed away.
So hidden from our sorrowing eyes,
Our young, sweet, spring-bloom buried lies;
One blast of earth swept o'er the flower,
It died, the blossom of an hour.

The Summer flowers are freshly blowing
  Beneath glad July's genial morn;
Like smiles the face of earth bestrowing,
  For fragrance and for beauty born;
My summer-flower has passed away,
'Tis now a blank, where all was gay;
A blank, where at each evening's close,
I hoped to watch my budding rose.

Soon Autumn, with overflowing measure,
 Will hang upon each bending tree
The clusters of its golden treasure,
 The life of earth's vast family.
Alas, in one disastrous hour,
From my green vine has fallen the flower ;
A blighted hue its branches wear,
My autumn tree looks cold and bare.

And Winter, with its blast wide-roaming,
 In cloud and darkness shall come forth ;
Beneath its grave of snow entombing
 The various verdure of the earth.
But my sweet blossom, safely laid,
Beneath you cloister's solemn shade,
In gentle undisturbed repose,
Shall sleep in winter's grave of snows.

CHOOSE WELL.

O quam dulce, quam jucundum
Erit tunc odisse mundum,
Et quam triste, quam amarum
Mundum habuisse carum.—OLD HYMN.

O DEAD in sin !
  Wilt thou still choose to die
  The death of deaths eternally ?
  Dost thou not feel the gloom
  Of the eternal tomb?

O dead to life !
  Wilt thou the life from heaven
  Reject? the life so freely given ;
  Wilt thou choose sin and tears
  Through everlasting years ?

O dead to Christ !
  Wilt thou despise the love
  Of Him who stooped from joy above,
  To shame on earth for thee,
  That he might set thee free ?

O dead to God !
Wilt thou not seek his face ?
Wilt thou not turn and own the grace !
Wilt thou not take the heaven,
So freely to thee given ?

'TWAS I THAT DID IT.

I SEE the crowd in Pilate's hall,
I mark their wrathful mien ;
Their shouts of " crucify" appall,
With blasphemy between.

And of that shouting multitude
I feel that I am one ;
And in that din of voices rude,
I recognise my own.

I see the scourges tear his back,
I see the piercing crown,
And of that crowd who smote and mock,
I feel that I am one,

Around yon cross, the throng I see,
  Mocking the sufferer's groan,
Yet still my voice it seems to be,—
  As if I mocked alone.

'Twas I that shed the sacred blood,
  I nailed him to the tree,
I crucified the Christ of God,
  I joined the mockery.

Yet not the less that blood avails,
  To cleanse away my sin,
And not the less that cross prevails
  To give me peace within.

THE USEFUL LIFE.

Ψυχή μου, ψυχή μου,
'Αναστα, τὶ καθευδεις.

OLD GREEK HYMN.

Go labor on ; spend, and be spent,—
  Thy joy to do the Father's will ;
It is the way the Master went,
  Should not the servant tread it still ?

Go labor on ; 'tis not for nought ;
  Thy earthly loss is heavenly gain ;
Men heed thee, love thee, praise thee **not ;**
  The Master praises,—what are men ?

Go labor on ; enough, while here,
  If He shall praise thee, if he deign
Thy willing heart to mark and cheer ;
  No toil for Him shall be in vain.

Go labor on; your hands are weak,
　　Your knees are faint, your soul cast down,
Yet falter not; the prize you seek,
　　Is near,—a kingdom and a crown !

Go labor on, while it is day,
　　The world's dark night is hastening on;
Speed, speed thy work, cast sloth away:
　　It is not thus that souls are won.

Men die in darkness at your side,
　　Without a hope to cheer the tomb;
Take up the torch and wave it wide,
　　The torch that lights time's thickest gloom.

Toil on, faint not, keep watch and pray;
　　Be wise the erring soul to win;
Go forth into the world's highway,
　　Compel the wanderer to come in.

Toil on, and in thy toil rejoice;
　　For toil comes rest, for exile home;
Soon shalt thou hear the Bridegroom's voice,
　　The midnight peal, behold I come !

PASSING THROUGH.

I WALK as one who knows that he is treading
   A stranger soil ;
As one round whom a serpent-world is spreading
   Its subtle coil.

I walk as one but yesterday delivered
   From a sharp chain ;
Who trembles lest the bond so newly severed
   Be bound again.

I walk as one who feels that he is breathing
   Ungenial air ;
For whom as wiles, the tempter still is wreathing
   The bright and fair.

My steps, I know, are on the plains of danger,
   For sin is near ;
But looking up, I pass along, a stranger,
   In haste and fear.

19*

This earth has lost its power to drag me downward;
　　　　Its spell is gone;
My course is now right upward, and right onward,
　　　　To yonder throne.

Hour after hour of time's dark night is stealing
　　　　In gloom away;
Speed thy fair dawn of light, and joy, and healing,
　　　　Thou Star of day!

For thee its God, its King, the long-rejected,
　　　　Earth groans and cries;
For thee the long-beloved, the long-expected,
　　　　Thy bride still sighs!

FORWARD.

SHALL this life of mine be wasted?
   * Shall this vineyard lie untilled?
Shall true joy pass by untasted,
     And this soul remain unfilled?

Shall the God-given hours be scattered,
     Like the leaves upon the plain? -
Shall the blossoms die unwatered
     By the drops of heavenly rain?

Shall I see each fair sun waking,
     And not feel, it wakes for me?
Each glad morning brightly breaking
     And not feel, it breaks for me?

Shall I see the roses blowing,
     And not wish to bloom as they?
Holy fragrance round me throwing,
     Luring others on the way.

Shall I hear the free bird singing
    In the summer's stainless sky,
Far aloft its glad flight winging,
    And not seek to soar as high ?

Shall this heart still spend its treasures
    On the things that fade and die;
Shall it court the hollow pleasures
    Of bewildering vanity ?

Shall these lips of mine be idle ;
    Shall I open them in vain ?
Shall I not with God's own bridle
    Their frivolities restrain ?

Shall these eyes of mine still wander ?—
    Or, no longer turned afar,
Fix a firmer gaze and fonder
    On the bright and morning Star ?

Shall these feet of mine, delaying,
    Still in ways of sin be found,
Braving snares and madly straying
    On the world's bewitching ground ?

No, I was not born to trifle
  Life away in dreams or sin!
No, I must not, dare not stifle
  Longings such as these within!

Swiftly moving, upward, onward,
  Let my soul in faith be borne;
Calmly gazing, skyward, sunward,
  Let my eye unshrinking turn!

Where the Cross, God's love revealing,
  Sets the fettered spirit free,
Where it sheds its wondrous healing,
  There, my soul, thy rest shall be!

Then no longer idly dreaming
  Shall I fling my years away;
But, each precious hour redeeming,
  Wait for the eternal day!

NOTHING BETWEEN.

FONDLY, fondly returneth the daylight
  To the old hill's grey peak ere the dawn has begun;
Slowly, slowly recedeth the daylight
  From the old hill's grey peak when the long day is
    done.

Softly, softly returneth the ripple
  To its rest on the sand of you green-margined bay,
Sadly, sadly recedeth the ripple
  To mingle again with the sea's drifting spray.

Gladly, gladly the dew of the twilight
  Floats up to the rainbow at blush of the dawn,
Slowly, slowly the dew of the twilight,
  Seeks the dark sod again when the sun is with-
    drawn.

It is thus, even thus, that the sunlight of heaven,
Returns and retires with the morn and the even;

Thus slowly retiring as sleep seals the eye,
Returning at day-spring with joy from on high.
Night's last gleam and truest, my God's gracious love,
Morn's first beam and fondest, his joy from above.

Yet, 'tis not night alone that comes between
My God and me, to mar the peaceful scene;
But the world's blazing day, hour after hour,
Beats on my head, and with its scorching power
Dries up my dew and sap, nay dims my eye
With its bewildering blaze of vanity.
Then comes the quiet and the cool of night,
To give me back the calm, of which the light
Of this gay world had sought me to bereave.
O gentle shadows of the tranquil eve!
Eve with thy stillness and soul-soothing balm,
What do I owe thee for thy solemn calm!
Thou comest down like some peace-bringing dove,
To soothe and cheer me with thy silent love.

FOLLOW THOU ME.

RESTORE to me the freshness of my youth,
　　And give me back my soul's keen edge again,
That time has blunted!　O, my early truth,—
　　Shall I not you regain?
Ah, mine has been a wasted life at best,
All unreality and long unrest;
　　Yes, I have lived in vain!

But now no more in vain;—my soul, awake,
　　Shake off the snare, untwist the fastening chain:
Arise, go forth, the selfish slumber break,
　　Thy idle dreams restrain!
Still half thy life before thee lies untrod,
Live for the endless living, live for God!—
　　I must not live in vain!

My God! the way is rough and sad the night,
　　And my soul faints and breathes this weeping strain,
And the world hates me with its bitterest spite,—
　　For I have left its train,

With thee and with thy saints to cast my lot:
Ah, my dear Lord, let me not be forgot,
Let me not live in vain !

Can we not part in silence, since for ever,
This world and I ? From scorn and taunt refrain ?
Must it still hate and wound ? still stir the fever
Of this poor throbbing brain ?
Ah, yes, it must be so, my God, my God;
'Tis the true discipline, the needed rod,
Else I should live in vain !

The foe is strong,—his venomed rage I dread,
Yet, O my God, do thou his wrath restrain ;
Shield me in battle, soothe my aching head
In the sharp hour of pain :
But more than this, oh give me toiling faith,
Large-hearted love, and zeal unto the death :
Let me not live in vain.

Restore to me the freshness of my youth,
And give me back my soul's keen edge again :
Ah, let my spring return ! bright hope and truth
Shall I not you regain ?

20

No wasted life, my God, shall mine now be,
Hours, days, and years filled up with toil for thee :
 I shall not live in vain !

VANITY.

Τε ἀληθως ἀγαθα οὐκ ἐστιν ἐν τῇ κατηραμενη γῃ.—ORIGEN

NAY 'tis not that we fancied it,
 This magic world of ours ;
We thought its skies were only blue,
 Its fields all sun and flowers.

Its streams all summer-bright and glad,
 Its seas all smiles and calms,
Its path from youth to age, one long
 Green avenue of palms.

But clouds came up with glooom and shade
 Our sky was overcast,
The hot mist threw its blight around,
 Sunshine and flowers went past.

Hopes perished, that had hung like wreaths
    Around youth's buoyant brow,
And joys, like withered autumn leaves,
    Dropped from the shaken bough.

Yet from these clouds comes forth the light,—
    Light beaming from on high;
And from these faded flowers spring up
    The flowers that can not die.

Far fairer is the land we seek,
    A land without a tomb,
An everlasting resting-place,
    A sure and quiet home.

Far sunnier than the hills of time
    Are its eternal hills;
Far fresher than the rills of earth
    Are its eternal rills.

No blight can fall upon its flowers,
    No darkness fill its air,
It has a day forever bright,
    For Christ, its sun, is there.

O Sun of love and peace, arise,
Thy light upon us beam;
For all this life is but a sleep,
And all this world a dream.

MACHPELAH.

ONLY a tomb, no more!
A rock-hewn sepulchre,
And this, and this is all that's thine,
Fair Canaan's mighty heir!

Only a tomb, no more!
A future resting-place,
When God shall lay thee down, and bid
All thy long wanderings cease.

This cave and field,—no more,—
Canst thou thy dwelling call;
That land of thine,—plains, hills, woods,
streams,—
The stranger has it all!

Thy altar and thy tent
  Are all that thou hast here:
With these content, thou passest on,
  A homeless wanderer.

Thy life unrest and toil;
  Thy course a pilgrimage;
Only in death thou goest down,
  To claim thy heritage;—

A heritage which death
  Shall seal to thee for aye,
A resurrection-heritage
  When all things pass away.

A home of endless peace,
  Beyond these hills of strife;
When these old rocks give up their dead,
  And death shall end in life.

A heritage of life,
  Beyond this guarded gloom,
A kingdom, not a field or cave;
  A city, not a tomb.

20*

OLD WORDS.

Ἁπλᾶ γάρ ἐστι τῆς ἀληθείας ἔπη.—ÆSCHYLUS.

WAS this earth sunnier in the days of old?
Or was it but the eye that looked on it,
That then was fresher, happier, in the youth
And manhood of our race? Were springs more bright
And summers levelier, lighted up by suns
Long set,—suns of a younger heaven than ours?
Was the air purer ere the heavy breath
Of ages had gone to poison it?
Did the long gleam upon the ancient Nile
Blaze in a richer radiance to the noon,
When History's old father gazed upon it?
Or was the sunshine on the hills of Greece
Purer when Homer sang and Sappho wept:
Or was the brow of Lebanon more fair
With whiter snow-wreaths, when the kings of Tyre
Builded their marble palaces beneath
The mighty shadows of its haughty peaks?

Was this earth sunnier in the days of old,
Or is the glory hovering o'er its hills,
And wandering thro' the unfathomable stretch
Of its old skies, of which men fondly tell,
But the gay vision of a fresher eye,
When this old race was younger, and men's steps
Went with more buoyant freedom over earth ?
Or was it all a dream, a dream of youth,
When dreams are happiest ?   Is it still a dream,
Well-dreamt in these our days, when men look out
With sad eye on the present, as if clouds,
Unknown in other days, had settled down
Upon our hills to shut out sun and stars ?
I know not.   Yet I love to wander back
To this earth's younger days and earlier scenes,
In which there seems to meet both age and youth,
The blossom and the fruit, the joy of dawn,
And the grave quiet of the solemn eve.

Was the world wiser in the days of old,
When in this land our fathers died for truth,
Or is the wisdom of these ancient times,
A fable well-devised, to keep us lowly ?
And are the words and thoughts of other days,
The martyr-words and thoughts, and above all

The martyr-deeds of mighty men whose hair
Grew grey before its time, whose youthful face
Grew early pale, and o'er whose thoughtful brow
Age drew its furrows, prematurely deep,—
Are these old words, and thoughts, and noble deeds
But meant for them who heard and saw them then,
But overdated now, unsuitable
For manhood and full age, like that to which
We have attained in these our riper times?
It cannot be so; truth is ever true,
In this age or the last, and error false,
To-day as it was yesterday.   No age
Can outgrow truth, or can afford to part
With the tried wisdom of the past, with words
That centuries have sifted, and on which
Ages have set their seal, and handed down
From venerable lips of solemn men,
Who learned their wisdom in a graver school,
And in an age of keener, sorer conflict
Than we have known in this gay holiday,
When truth and error are but things of taste,
Changelings of fashion, altering year by year.

Guard then those ancient wells, those living springs,
Of which our fathers drank and were refreshed.

Guard then these ancient palms beneath whose shade
Our fathers have sat down, and of whose fruit
They ate and went upon their way in peace.
Part not with these old names, each one of which
Bears in its bosom precious histories,
The life-deeds and death-conflicts of the men
From out whose loins we spring, the men of might
And wisdom, who have won such victories
Of truth for us.   These venerable names
And words preserve, as an inheritance
For children's children to the latest age.
Part not with these old names and words, each one
Contains an everlasting history,—
A great soul's history, which like a pearl
Within its shell lies hid.   Fling not away
The shell because unpolished and uncouth,
Lest in so doing thou shouldst fling away
The gem whose lustre lies unseen within.
   It is not beauty, it is truth we seek,
And it is truth that men would fling away,
Because its outward garb is rude and homely.
Yet truth is beauty, best of beauty here;   —
And beauty is but hidden truth unfolded,
Like blossoms from the rough brown buds of spring.

Part not with these old names.   See how they shine
In these old heavens, like stars, whose rays no age
Can dim, nor boastful art of man supplant,
By lights, the invention of his fruitful skill.
They lighted up the darkness of the ways
By which our fathers walked in joy to heaven ;
Not now less needful nor less glad their beams.
Part not with these old names and words, each one
Is as a seed, the womb of hidden life ;
And he that flings away a seed destroys
The future harvest of a hundred fields.
Part not with these old names, in each of them
Our fathers wrapt up wisdom for their sons,
And their sons' sons down to earth's latest day.
What thoughts are clinging round them, thick as dew
Upon the fields of the fresh summer's grass,
Mellow as fruit upon the autumn-trees.
    Say not, our age is wiser; if it be,
It is the wisdom which the past has given
That makes it so ; for in these names is written
That wondrous wisdom that has made us wise.

THE OLD JEW ON MOUNT MORIAH.

He stood bewildered on his lonely hearth,
  Sadness was written on his fixéd brow,
For he had witnessed days of holy mirth
  Where silence dwells and desolation now.
  The grief he felt he cared not to avow.
Calmly he stood, yet sorrowfully too,
  The latest leaf upon the topmost bough
Of the green olive that so lately threw
Aloft its leafy arms when the glad spring was new

Friendless and homeless ! How unlike the past !
  Once honored scion of a noble stem ;
But now forsaken, desolate, the last
  Bright jewel of a kingly diadem ;
  The last dim dew-drop of all those that gem
The still lone valley where the sunbeams fall.
  He trod his ancient hills, but found on them
Nought but his shivered altar-shrines, for all
Was tomb-like hushed, and dark as with a funeral
      pall.

THE SHEPHERDS' PLAIN.

'Dum servant *oves* invenerunt *Agnum* Dei."—JEROME.

BLESSED night, when first that plain
Echoed with the joyful strain,—
" Peace has come to earth again."

Blessed hills, that heard the song
Of the glorious angel-throng,
Swelling all your slopes along.

Happy shepherds, on whose ear
Fell the tidings glad and dear,—
" God to man is drawing near."

Happy shepherds, on whose eye
Shone the glory from on high,
Of the heavenly Majesty.

Happy, happy Bethlehem,
Judah's least but brightest gem,
Where the rod from Jesse's stem.

Scion of a princely race,
Sprung in heaven's own perfect grace,
Yet in feeble lowliness.

This the woman's promised seed,
Abram's mighty son indeed ;
Succorer of earth's great need.

This the victor in our war,
This the glory seen afar,
This the light of Jacob's star !

Happy Judah, rise and own
Him, the heir of David's throne,
David's Lord, and David's Son.

Babe of promise, born at last,
After weary ages past,
When our hopes were overcast.

21

Babe of weakness, can it be,
That earth's last great victory
Is to be achieved by thee ?

Child of meekness, can it be
That the proud rebellious knee
Of this world shall bend to thee ?

Child of poverty, art thou
He to whom all heaven shall bow,
And all earth shall pay the vow ?

Can that feeble head alone
Bear the weight of such a crown,
As belongs to David's Son ?

Can these helpless hands of thine,
Wield a sceptre so divine,
As belongs to Jesse's line ?

Heir of pain and toil, whom none
In this evil day will own,
Art thou the Eternal One ?

Thou, o'er whom the sword and rod
Wave, in haste, to drink thy blood,
Art thou very Son of God?

Thus revealed to shepherds' eyes,
Hidden from the great and wise,
Entering earth in lowly guise,—

Entering by this narrow door,
Laid upon this rocky floor,
Placed in yonder manger poor.

We adore thee as our King,
And to thee our song we sing;
Our best offering to thee bring.

Guarded by the shepherds' rod,
'Mid their flock, thy poor abode,
Thus we own thee, Lamb of God.

Lamb of God, thy lowly name,
King of kings, we thee proclaim;
Heaven and earth shall hear its fame.

Bearer of our sins' sad load,
Wielder cf the iron rod,
Judah's Lion, Lamb of God !

Mighty King of righteousness,
King of glory, king of peace,
Never shall thy kingdom cease !

Thee, earth's heir and Lord, we own :
Raise again its fallen throne,
Take its everlasting crown.

Blessed Babe of Bethlehem,
Owner of earth's diadem,
Claim, and wear the radiant gem.

Scatter darkness with thy light,
End the sorrows of our night,
Speak the word, and all is bright.

Spoil the spoiler of the earth,
Bring creation's second birth,
Promised day of song and mirth

'Tis thine Israel's voice that calls,
Build again thy Salem's walls,
Dwell within her holy halls.

-'Tis thy Church's voice that cries,
Rend these long unrended skies,
Bridegroom of the Church, arise.

Take to thee thy power and reign,
Purify this earth again;
Cleanse it from each curse and stain.

Sun of peace, no longer stay,
Let the shadows flee away,
And the long night end in day.

Let the dayspring from on high,
That arose in Judah's sky,
Cover earth eternally.

Babe of Bethlehem, to thee,
Infant of eternity,
Everlasting glory be !
21*

COME, LORD.

"Senuit mundus."—AUGUSTINE.

COME, Lord, and tarry not:
   Bring the long-looked-for day,
Oh why these years of waiting here,
   These ages of delay?

Come, for thy saints still wait;
   Daily ascends their sigh;
The Spirit and the Bride say, Come,
   Dost thou not hear the cry?

Come, for creation groans,
   Impatient of thy stay,
Worn out with these long years of ill,
   These ages of delay.

Come, for thy Israel pines,
   An exile from thy fold;
O call to mind thy faithful word,
   And bless them as of old.

Come, for thy foes are strong;
   With taunting lip they say,
" Where is the promised Advent now,
   And where the dreaded day ?"

Come, for the good are few;
   They lift the voice in vain,
Faith waxes fainter on the earth,
   And love is on the wane.

Come, for the truth is weak,
   And error pours abroad
Its subtle poison o'er the earth,—
   An earth that hates her God.

Come, for love waxes cold,
   Its steps are faint and slow;
Faith now is lost in unbelief,
   Hope's lamp burns dim and low.

Come, for the grave is full,
   Earth's tombs no more can hold,
The sated sepulchres rebel,
   And groans the heaving mould.

Come, for the corn is ripe,
   Put in thy sickle now,
Reap the great harvest of the earth ;—
   Sower and reaper thou !

Come, in thy glorious might,
   Come with the iron rod,
Scattering thy foes before thy face,
   Most mighty Son of God.

Come, spoil the strong man's house,
   Bind him and cast him hence,
Show thyself stronger than the strong,
   Thyself Omnipotence.

Come, and make all things new,
   Build up this ruined earth,
Restore our faded Paradise,
   Creation's second birth.

Come, and begin thy reign
   Of everlasting peace,
Come, take the kingdom to thyself,
   Great King of righteousness.

THY WAY, NOT MINE.

Thy way, not mine, O Lord,
    However dark it be!
Lead me by thine own hand,
    Choose out the path for me.

Smooth let it be or rough,
    It will be still the best,
Winding or straight, it matters not,
    It leads me to thy rest.

1 dare not choose my lot:
    I would not, if I might;
Choose thou for me, my God,
    So shall I walk aright.

The kingdom that I seek
    Is thine: so let the way
That leads to it be thine,
    Else I must surely stray.

Take thou my cup, and it
  With joy or sorrow fill, —
As best to thee may seem ;
  Choose thou my good and ill.

Choose thou for me my friends,
  My sickness or my health,
Choose thou my cares for me,
  My poverty or wealth.

Not mine, not mine the choice,
  In things or great or small ;
Be thou my guide, my strength,
  My wisdom, and my all.

ALLELUIA.

(FROM THE LATIN.)

ALLELUIA, Alleluia!
    The battle now is done,
    The victory is won;
    Let us joy and sing
Alleluia!

Alleluia, Alleluia!
    Suffering death's cruel doom,
    Jesus hath hell overcome;
    Let us praise and shout
Alleluia!

Alleluia, Alleluia!
    He rose the third day, bright
    In heavenly love and light;
    Let us cry and chant
Alleluia!

Alleluia, Alleluia !
>Closed are the gates below,
>Heaven's halls are open now ;
>Let us joy and sing
Alleluia !

Alleluia, Alleluia !
>Jesus, by thy wounds, save
>Us from the endless grave,
>That we may live and sing
Alleluia ! *

---

* I give the first stanza of the above hymn as a specimen

>Alleluia, Alleluia !
>>Finita jam sunt prælia,
>>Est parta jam victoria,
>>Gaudeamus et canamus,
>>>Alleluia !

LIVE.

Make haste, O man, to live,
 For thou so soon must die;
Time hurries past thee like the breeze;
 How swift its moments fly.
    Make haste, O man, to live!

To breathe, and wake, and sleep,
 To smile, to sigh, to grieve;
To move in idleness through earth,
 This, this is not to live!
    Make haste, O man, to live!

Make haste, O man, to do
 Whatever must be done;
Thou hast no time to lose in sloth,
 Thy day will soon be gone.
    Make haste, O man, to live!

Up then with speed, and work ;
　　Fling ease and self away ;
This is no time for thee to sleep,
　　Up, watch, and work and pray !
　　　　　　　Make haste, O man, to live

The useful, not the great,
　　The thing that never dies ;
The silent toil that is not lost,—
　　Set these before thine eyes.
　　　　　　　Make haste, O man, to live !

The seed, whose leaf and flower,
　　Though poor in human sight,
Brings forth at last the eternal fruit,
　　Sow thou by day and night.
　　　　　　　Make haste, O man, to live !

Make haste, O man, to live,
　　Thy time is almost o'er ;
O sleep not, dream not, but arise,
　　The Judge is at the door.
　　　　　　　Make haste, O man, to live !

THE MARTYR'S GRAVE.

THE moss is green upon the stone;
   The stone lies heavy on the mould;
The spot is dreary, sad, and lone;
   The forest air is cold.

The sky above is wan and bleak;
   The ground beneath is brown and bare;
No living voice intrudes to break
   The tranquil silence there.

Another breeze among the boughs,
   And then another leafy shower
Comes rustling down; the sadness grows
   More and more sad each hour.

The shadow of the drifting cloud
   Falls chilly on these gloomy firs,
Deepening the darkness of the wood;
   Hardly a leaflet stirs.

Quick-twinkling through the leafy screen,
  The stray gleams go and come ;
Half-hidden by the shade, is seen
  The old and well-known tomb.

Here sleeps the martyr's weary head ;
  Here moulders holy dust,
With the wild wood-moss overspread,
  Resting in silent trust.

No summer-flowers breathe sweetness here,
  It is a lone forsaken spot,
Round lie the leaves of autumn sere,
  The leaf that changes not.

Far from man's voice of love or strife,
  'Tis fit that here his grave should be,
In death an outcast as in life—
  Unnamed in history.

Young hopes, young friendships, joys of earth,
  Had passed him by like summer-dreams,
Solemn his life had been from birth,
  Like march of mountain streams.

Changeful his lot, like yon vexed sky,
　　When moorland breezes wildly blow,
His weary soul now rests on high,
　　His body sleeps below.

Rest, weary dust, lie here an hour;
　　Ere long, like blossom from the sod,
Thou shalt come forth a glorious flower,
　　Fit for the eye of God.

22*

ALL WELL.

No seas again shall sever;
　　No desert intervene;
No deep and flowing river
　　Shall roll its tide between.

No bleak cliffs upward towering,
　　Shall bound our eager sight;
No tempest darkly lowering,
　　Shall wrap us in its night.

Love, and unsevered union
　　Of soul with those we love,
Nearness and glad communion
　　Shall be our joy above.

No dread of wasting sickness,
　　No thought of ache or pain,
No fretting hours of weakness,
　　Shall mar our peace again.

No death our homes o'ershading,
   Shall e'er our harps unstring,
For all is life unfading,
   In presence of our King.

LINKS.

ARE there not voices, strangely sweet,
   And tones of music strangely dear;
So lovingly the soul they greet,
   So kindly steal they on the ear.

We know not why they strike so deep,
   We can not tell the secret spring
Within us, which they wake from sleep,
   Nor how such thoughts their notes can bring.

We ask not why nor how they thrill
   So keenly through the inmost soul;
And why, when ceased, we listen still,
   As though they yet upon us stole.

We feel the sweetness of the voice;
   We love the richness of the tone;
It makes us sorrow or rejoice,
   Compelling us its power to own.

Are there not words, too, strangely sweet,
   Thoughts, musings, memories, strangely dear?
So lovingly the soul they greet,
   So gently steal they on the ear!

Common the words may be and weak,
   The passing stranger owns them not;
To other ears in vain they speak,
   Unknown, unrelished, or forgot.

Rich in old thoughts, these words appear,
   Part of our being's mighty whole;
Linked with our life's strange story here,
   Knit to each feeling of our soul.

Linked with the scenes of days gone past,
   With all life's earnest hopes and fears;
Linked with the smiles that did not last,
   The joys and griefs of faded years.

Linked with old dreams once dreamt in youth,
  When dreams were gladder, truer things;
When each night's vision of bright truth,
  Lent to each buoyant day its wings.

Linked with the whisper of the trees,
  When summer eves were fair and still;
Set to the music of the breeze,
  Or murmur of the twilight rill.

Linked with some scene of sacred calm,
  Of holy places, holy days;
Linked with the prayer, the hymn, the psalm,
  The multitude's glad voice of praise.

Linked with the names of holy men,
  Martyr, or saint, or brother dear;
Some parted, ne'er to meet again,
  Some still our fellow-pilgrims here.

Linked with that name of names, the name
  Of Him who bought us with his blood;
Who bore for us the wrath and shame,
  The Virgin's Son, the Christ of God.

THE RESURRECTION OF THE JUST.

Autumn has come at last; and nature now
Binds up her summer tresses and disrobes,
That she may lay herself in silence down
Upon her winter's couch, and thereby sleep,
Repair her worn-out energies, and draw
New life into her veins, that when the sun
Flames out again, and the long-silent voice
Of happy birds and happier children wakes
Spring's first glad matin song, she may arise
Girt with new strength and with fresh beauty clothed.
Thus comes life's autumn, and the happy spirit,
Calmly disrobing, lays its garments down
Upon the leaf-strewn soil of this old earth,
Committing them, in quiet confidence
To the safe keeping of the trusty tomb,
Till death's brief winter shall have passed away.
Then these old robes with which she walked the earth,
Purged from each stain of vile mortality
By the all-cleansing winter of the grave,

And blanched to glorious whiteness by its gloom,
Shall shine in fairer, fresher purity,
When earth's long-promised spring at last arrives,
And the unsetting sun smiles down in peace
O'er a new paradise of love and joy.

THE PRAYER.

FETCH me the lightning from yon frowning cloud,
  With fiery force to break or melt this heart,—
A heart all earthly, foolish, vain, and proud;
  In unbelief and hate that bids its God depart.

Fetch me a beam from yon clear star of night;
  Or yet a warmer ray from day's bright sun,
To kindle into heat, and glow, and light,
  This soul of gloom and death, whose day seems
    scarce begun.

Fetch me a drop from yon translucent lake,
  Or, farther up, from yon pure mountain well,
These lips to cool, this feverish thirst to slake,
  This weary frame to freshen, these fierce fires to
    quell.

O thou my God, my being's health and source,
  Better than life, brighter than noon to me,
Stretch out thy loving hand, with gentle force,
  Bend this still-struggling will, and draw it after
    Thee.

Return to me, my oft-forgotten God,
  My spirit's true though long-forsaken rest;
Undo these bars, re-enter thine abode,
  In Thee and in Thy love alone would I be blest.

Re-mould this inner man in every part,
  Re-knit these broken ties, resume thy sway;
Take, as Thy throne and altar, this poor heart;
  Oh teach me how to love, oh help me to obey!

THE CITY.

Thou art no child of the city;
  Hadst thou known it as I have done,
Thou wouldst not have smiled with pity,
  As if joy were with thee alone.

With thee the unfettered ranger
  Of the forest and moorland free;
As if gloom and toil and danger
  Could alone in a city be.

The smoke, the din, and the bustle
  Of the city, I know them well,
And I know the gentle rustle
  Of the leaves in your breezy dell.

Day's hurry, and evening's riot,
  In the city I know them all;
I know, too, the loving quiet
  Of your glen at the day's sweet fall.

23

I know too each grim old alley,
  With the blanched ray flickering through;
I know each sweep of your valley,
  Where the rosy light lies in dew.

I know too the stifling sadness
  Of the summer-noon's sultry street;
I 've breathed the air of your gladness
  Where the streams and the breezes meet.

I know the dun haunts of fever,
  Where the blossoms of youth decay;
I know where your free broad river
  Sweeps disease on its breast away.

Yet despite your earnest pity,
  And despite its own smoke and din,
I cling to yon crowded city,
  Though I shrink from its woe and sin.

For I know its boundless measure,
  Of the true, and the good, and fair;
Its vast and far gathered treasure,
  All the wealth of soul that is there.

You may smile, or sneer, or pity,
    You may fancy it weak and strange ;
My eye to yon smoky city,
    Still returns from its widest range.

My heart in its inmost beatings
    Ever lingers around its homes ;
My soul wakes up in its greetings,
    To the gleam of its spires and domes.

You call it life's weary common,
    At the best but an idle fair,
The market of man and woman,—
    But the choice of the race are there.

The wonders of life and gladness,
    All the wonders of hope and fear;
The wonders of death and sadness,
    All the wonders of time are there.

In your lone lake's still face yonder,
    By your rivulet's bursting glee,
Deep truth I may read and ponder,
    Of the earth and its mystery.

THE CITY.

There seems, in yon city's motion,
    Yet a mightier truth for me;
'T is the sound of life's great ocean,
    'T is the tides of the human sea.

O'er the fields of earth lie scattered,
    Noble fruitage and blossoms rare;
Yon city the store has gathered,
    And the garner of hearts is there.

You may prize the lonely lustre
    Of your pearl or emerald green;
What is that to the gorgeous cluster
    On the brow of the crowned Queen?

And the home to which I 'm hasting,
    Is not in some silent glen;
The place where my hopes are resting,
    Is a city of living men.

The crowds are there; but the sadness
    Is fled, with the toil and pain;
Nought is heard but the song of gladness,—
    'T is the city of holy men.

And wilt thou my sad fate pity,
   Wilt thou grieve o'er my heavy doom
When within that resplendent city
   I shall find my glorious home?

THE END.